SHARP MICROWAVE OVEN TEST KITCHEN

Dear Sharp Customer:

We sincerely hope you will enjoy your new Sharp Microwave/Jet Convection Oven and the exciting world of microwave cooking. This cookbook will help you explore the many benefits of Microwave Convection Cooking and make meal preparation easier and more convenient than ever before possible.

Please read your cookbook thoroughly. Recipes from all categories of food preparation—family favourites to gourmet recipes—are included, as well as basic information on microwave cooking. The versatility of your Sharp Microwave Convection Oven is apparent by just scanning the Table of Contents.

Use your Sharp Microwave Convection Oven every time you prepare a meal. It saves time, energy, and is easy to operate. As you become better acquainted with your new oven, you will find additional uses for it and learn to easily convert your own favourite recipes to microwave and convection cooking.

Feel free to share your ideas with us. We will be happy to hear from you. When writing, please indicate the model number of your oven, your complete mailing address and telephone number.

If we can be of any further assistance, do not hesitate to contact us. We are pleased that you chose a Sharp product and hope you will enjoy using it.

Sincerely,

Sharp Home Economist

**SHARP MICROWAVE OVEN
TEST KITCHEN
SHARP HOUSE
THORP ROAD
NEWTON HEATH
MANCHESTER**

CONTENTS

Recipes **57**

MICROWAVE COOKING

Microwaves and other ultra-high frequency radio waves operate a variety of familiar systems, such as mobile telephones, remote control toys, air traffic control radar and remote television tuners.

What are Microwaves?

Microwaves are a form of high frequency radio waves similar to those used by a radio. However they are much shorter than radio waves.

At the heart of every microwave oven there is a magnetron which converts electrical energy into microwaves. These are transmitted into the oven via the wave guide where the microwaves are reflected, transmitted and absorbed.

Reflection

Microwaves cannot penetrate metal and are therefore reflected from the metal walls. Metal Cooking Utensils cannot be used as the microwaves will be reflected by the utensil and cannot penetrate the food.

Transmission

Microwaves pass through certain materials such as glass, china, plastic and paper. These materials do not reflect or absorb the microwaves and so are ideal materials for use as cooking materials.

Absorption

Microwaves are absorbed by food. The microwaves penetrate the food to a depth of about 2-to-4cm. (¾'' to 1½''). Microwave energy agitates the molecules of water, fat and sugar within the food. This causes vibration of the molecules at about 2½ billion times a second. Friction between the molecules produce heat in the food. When large items of food are being cooked frictional heat is conducted through to the centre of the food. This conducted heat process also continues during standing time.

Because microwaves dissipate as they are absorbed by the food they cannot be stored within the food.

Getting to Know your Microwave

When you first get your microwave oven it is important to sit down and read your operation manual and the Basics of Microwave cooking that are in this book. It will help you understand how your microwave works, what foods cook best in your microwave, how to defrost and reheat foods and how to get the best results from your microwave oven.

Always start by cooking simple things. Once these are mastered you will be able to try more advanced dishes.

The first time you use your microwave oven don't try to cook a complete meal in it. Incorporate it gradually into your routine and soon you'll be cooking meals and wondering how you ever managed before you had your microwave oven.

Advantages of the Turntable

The energy in a microwave oven is not distributed equally throughout the cavity. Some areas are warmer than others, with the consequence that food in those areas becomes hotter.

Stirring helps equalize heat in the food, but there are many foods which cannot be stirred. These foods must be rearranged or rotated if they are to cook evenly. The more often they are moved, the better the results.

The turntable is dishwasher-safe and rotates constantly while the food cooks, so no part of it remains in a warm area for any length of time. The turntable simplifies cooking, especially of foods which require frequent rotating, because it moves the food automatically.

The construction of the oven and the turntable may differ with each model.

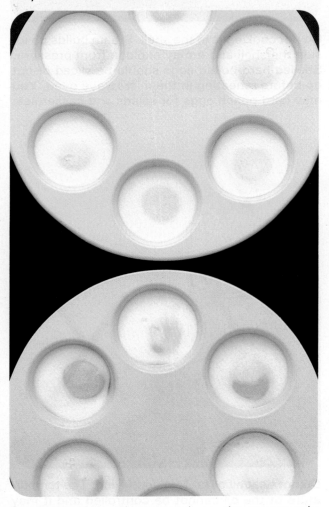

Compare eggs microwaved on the constantly rotating turntable (above) with unevenly cooked eggs microwaved in another oven (below).

Microwave Myths

Not everything you may have heard about microwave cooking is true. A number of myths persist because many people don't really understand how the microwave oven works. As you use your oven, you'll discover that some of them are half-truths, while others are entirely false.

MYTH 1. Microwaves cook from the inside out. They certainly do not. Microwaves penetrate foods from the outside to a depth of about 2—4cm (¾''—1½''). Small foods, under 5cm (2'') in diameter, are penetrated to the center from all sides. With larger foods, energy creates heat in the outer layer; then the heat moves to the centre by conduction, as it does conventionally. A few foods may appear to cook more on the inside. One example is an egg. Energy penetrates to the centre, where the fatty yolk becomes hotter than the white and cooks first.

MYTH 2. You can't use metal in a microwave oven. False. Metal reflects microwaves; the oven itself is made of metal so microwave energy can't escape. Inside the oven, metal slows cooking because it keeps energy from reaching parts of the food. You can use the reflective properties of metal to protect foods which might overcook in some areas. The magnetrons in most microwave ovens are designed so that they cannot be damaged by the use of metal in the oven.

MYTH 3. Dishes don't get hot in a microwave oven. Keep your pot holders handy. A microwave-safe utensil will not be heated by microwave energy, but it will become hot from contact with hot food. Heat tends to equalize. A warm object heats the air around it, like a radiator in a cool room. When food becomes hot, some of this heat is transferred to the dish.

MYTH 4. Microwaved foods don't stay hot. Not so. They cool at the same rate as conventionally heated foods, and for the same reason. No matter how you heat foods, they cool faster if you serve them in a cool dish. One advantage of microwaving is that you can cook and serve in the same dish, so food stays hot longer.

MYTH 5. Foods don't brown in a microwave oven. True and false. Browning depends on fat content and the amount of cooking time in relation to food volume. Some foods do brown: bacon, roast, a turkey. Many small, moist foods cook so rapidly they do not have time to brown.

Do's and Don't's

The purpose of this book is to show you what the microwave oven can do. You'll find many delicious, attractive foods you may not have known you could prepare by microwaving. Each section provides explanations of what you should do, and why, so you cook with confidence.

Read the Operation Manual for information on operating and cleaning. Do not remove the turntable while oven is in use.

Humidity and moisture in the food will influence the amount of condensation in your oven. Covered foods cause less condensation than uncovered foods. Condensation is normal in microwave cooking. Be sure the vent of your oven is not blocked.

The door seal on your oven is designed to prevent the leakage of microwave energy during cooking. Occasionally moisture may appear around the oven door. You may also see some small areas of light or feel warm air around the door. None of these situations are abnormal and do not indicate that your oven is leaking microwave energy.

Do not cook eggs in the shell. Steam builds up inside the shell and it may explode from pressure. Shelled hard-boiled eggs should be sliced or cut up before reheating in the microwave oven. You may hard-poach eggs for salads and casseroles.

Pop popcorn only in special microwave poppers, following manufacturer's directions. Do not use oil unless specified by the manufacturer, or heat longer than recommended. Never pop popcorn in paper bags or glass utensils.

Do not heat oil or fat for deep-frying. The temperature of the oil cannot be controlled and it may overheat. Do not attempt to can in the microwave oven as it requires prolonged high temperatures.

Microwave Utensils

The ideal material for a microwave utensil is transparent to microwaves; it allows energy to pass through the container and heat the food. Many ordinary household items, such as paper, plastic or wooden bowls may be used to warm foods to serving temperature.

When a utensil is used for cooking, it must also be able to withstand contact with very hot food or boiling liquid. Manufacturers are now marketing dual-purpose, heat-resistant paper and plastic utensils which can be used in both microwave and conventional ovens; in addition, many traditional cooking containers are suitable for microwaving.

Read this section, then check your cupboards. You may already have microwave oven-safe utensils. If you are not sure, use this test: place the empty dish in the oven; microwave at HIGH (100%) 30 seconds. A dish which becomes very hot should not be used.

Useful for meat cooking are a 30x20 cm utility dish or a 25 cm casserole and a rack or trivet to fit. Oven glass cups and batter bowls can be used for both measuring and cooking. Ring shapes are ideal. Make your own by placing a glass in a 2½ to 3-litre casserole. Cook some foods directly on the turntable.

Paper plates and hot drink cups may be used for heating. Paper baking cases absorb excess moisture from cupcakes or miffins and save clean-up. Heat breads or cook bacon on paper towels. Cook frozen vegetables in their bags. Cover foods with kitchen paper to prevent spatters.

Ovenable paper containers come in a variety of shapes and sizes. They are freezer-proof and safe for both microwaving and conventional ovens up to 200°C.

Oven glass utensils are inexpensive and widely available. Use them for measuring, mixing and microwaving. Choose clear glass for pies, cakes and breads, so you can check for doneness through the bottom of the dish.

Glass ceramic utensils can be used for microwaving and serving, as well as on range tops or in conventional ovens.

Browning utensils are made of glass-ceramic and are coated on the bottom with a material which absorbs microwave energy. After the empty dish is preheated in the microwave oven, it sears and browns the surface of foods. The dish cannot be used for conventional cooking, with certain types of browning dishes on insulating rack is advisable.

Pottery, stoneware and porcelain serving bowls, platters, casseroles, plates, and cups make attractive microwave cook-and-serve ware. Many are labeled, ''Microwave safe.'' If you are not sure, use the dish test.

Usable metal includes aluminum foil for shielding, and shallow foil convenience food trays. The amount of metal used must be in proportion to the volume of food; foil trays should be two-thirds to three-fourths full. The foil should not touch the walls of the oven.

Keep metal at least 2.5cm (1'') away from oven walls. Deep trays and metal pans are unsuitable because they reflect too much energy away from food. Foil-lined cartons shield food completely, so it does not heat at all.

Plastic film cooking bags and boiling bags are ideal for microwaving. Do not use metal closures. Food storage bags should not be used for cooking. Plastic film makes a convenient cover for baking dishes; vent it so steam escapes.

Plastic cookware of polysulfone and thermoset-filled polyesters withstand high food temperatures. Follow manufacturers' recommendations for use with specific foods.

Styrofoam® and ''dishwasher safe'' plastic storage containers and tableware may be used for heating foods to serving temperature. Do not use them for cooking raw foods, or for heating foods high in fat or sugar content, since they distort at fairly low temperatures.

Do not use dishes with metallic trim; utensils with metal screws, bands or handles; Melamine® tableware; delicate glassware or plastics which may be sensitive to hot foods; cups or mugs with handles repaired with glue; conventional meat or candy thermometers.

Microwave Cooking Principles

The speed and evenness of microwave cooking is affected by the foods themselves. Microwaves penetrate foods to a depth of 2 to 4cm on all surfaces: top, bottom, and sides. The interior of foods greater than 5cm in diameter heats by conduction, as it does in conventional cooking. Foods with high water, fat or sugar content respond quickly to microwave energy. Understanding the way food characteristics influence cooking will help you enjoy the benefits of microwaving.

Quantity. Microwave cooking times are directly related to the amount of food in the oven. Because energy is absorbed by the food itself, one potato or a single piece of chicken cooks rapidly. When the energy is divided among several items, cooking takes more time.

Size. Small pieces cook faster than large ones. To speed cooking, cut pieces smaller than 5 cm, so microwaves can penetrate to the centre from all sides. For even cooking, make all the pieces the same size.

Shape. Foods which are irregular in shape, like fish fillets, chicken breasts or drumsticks, take longer to cook in the thicker parts. To help them cook evenly, place the thickest parts to the outside of the dish, where they will receive more energy.

Starting Temperature. Frozen or refrigerated food takes longer to heat than food at room temperature. Cooking times in this book are based on normal storage temperatures. Since rooms, refrigerators, and freezers differ in temperature, check for doneness at the minimum time.

Moisture Content. Microwaves are attracted by moisture. Naturally moist foods microwave better than dry ones. Add a minimum of liquid to moist foods, as excess water slows cooking. Prick foods with skins like those on potatoes or squash, so internal steam can escape.

Fat and Bone. Marbling within meat, or a thin, even layer of fat on a roast, speeds cooking. Large fatty areas or excess drippings in dish attract energy away from the meat and slow cooking. Centre bones do not affect cooking, but bone on the side of meat conducts heat to the areas next to it.

Density. The depth to which microwaves penetrate foods varies depending on their density. Porous foods, like minced beef or mashed potatoes, microwave faster than dense ones like steak or whole potatoes.

Microwave Cooking Techniques

Many of the techniques of microwaving are similar to those used in conventional cooking. They help equalize energy in the food so that it cooks evenly. Some techniques also shorten cooking time, so you get the full benefit of microwave speed.

Depth of food in dish affects both speed and evenness of cooking. Food in a shallow casserole will cook faster than food in a deep dish of the same capacity. Choose casseroles with straight sides; in a dish with sloping sides, the outside top edges receive more energy and overcook.

Ring shapes are ideal for microwaving because energy penetrates food from top, bottom, sides and centre. Round shapes cook more evenly than squares or rectangles, which absorb most energy in the corners.

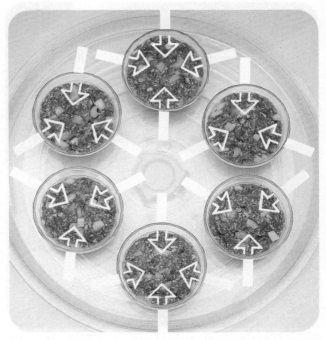

Arrange individual items, like custard cups or baked potatoes, in a ring around the outside of the turntable. Leave space between foods so energy can penetrate them from all sides.

Arrange foods with thin or delicate ends, like drumsticks or asparagus spears, with the thick or tougher portions to the outside of the dish. The parts which need more cooking will receive more energy, so food will microwave evenly.

Shield areas which attract the most energy, like the wing tips or breast bone of a turkey or corners of a square cake. Use small pieces of foil, which reflect microwaves. Covering meats with a sauce also acts as a shield to prevent drying.

Covering the dish holds in heat and steam to speed cooking. Use a casserole lid or plastic wrap. Vent plastic by turning back one edge at the side of dish to form a narrow slot where excess steam can escape. To hold in heat and prevent spatters without steaming, use waxed paper.

Paper toweling placed under breads, crackers, or crumb-coated chicken pieces absorbs moisture from steam which builds up between food and turntable, keeping surfaces crisp and dry. Cover foods with paper toweling to prevent spatters.

Microwave Cooking Techniques (continued)

Stir foods from outside to centre of dish once or twice during cooking to equalize heat and speed microwaving. Foods will not scorch or stick, so there's no need to stir constantly as you do in conventional cooking.

Turn foods over once during microwaving to speed cooking of medium-sized pieces, like chicken and hamburgers. Large items like turkeys and roasts must be turned over because areas near the top of the oven receive most energy.

Rearrange overlapping areas, like tails of long fish fillets, from top to bottom, and closely packed pieces, like meat balls, from the outside to the centre of the dish. Rotating or repositioning dish in the energy pattern is not needed with the turntable.

Lower power levels cycle energy on and off to equalize heat in foods. When energy is off, heat spreads by conduction from warm to cool areas. Sensitive foods don't overheat, and less tender meats have time to tenderize.

Standing time is one of the most important microwaving techniques. Heat is in the food, not the oven, and many foods build up enough internal heat so they continue to cook by themselves after they are removed from the oven. Letting roasts, large whole vegetables and cakes stand to finish cooking allows the centre to cook completely without overcooking, drying or toughening the outsides. It also saves energy and money.

Browning develops on roasts and turkeys or chops, steaks and hamburgers microwaved in a browning utensil. Other foods will look cooked but not brown. Browning agents do not affect the quality of microwaved foods, but can add colour and flavour. For meats and poultry, soy, Worcestershire, barbecue or steak sauce; a sprinkling of paprika or dry gravy mix; or crumb coating. Frostings and toppings finish cakes and breads. Top casseroles at the end of microwaving with grated cheese or crumbs.

Variable Cooking Control

The Variable Cooking Control on Sharp Microwave Ovens adds a new dimension to microwave cooking. It is now possible to select the speed at which you cook foods in your microwave oven, just as you control the rate of cooking on your conventional cooker. The Variable Cooking Control lets you defrost, simmer, roast or cook at HIGH to give each food the proper amount of microwave energy for best results.

To understand how to use the Variable Cooking Control, you need to know how it works. The microwave energy cycles switch on and off at various intervals to allow you to control the rate of heating and cooking. There are five settings: HIGH, MEDIUM HIGH, MEDIUM, MEDIUM LOW and LOW.

Variable Cooking Control Setting	Appriximate Percentage of Microwave Power	
HIGH	(Full Power)	100%
MEDIUM HIGH	(Roast)	70%
MEDIUM	(Simmer)	50%
MEDIUM LOW	(Defrost)	30%
LOW	(Warm)	10%

The Variable Cooking Control, is easy to use. After you have set the desired cooking time, select the Variable Cooking Control setting you need.

In all probability the speed and convenience of microwave cooking were you major reasons for purchasing your Sharp Microwave Oven. You will find that most foods are cooked on HIGH or MED HIGH. In either case most foods can be cooked in about a quarter of their conventional times using these settings. Other foods traditionally require long, slow cooking for tenderness or to develop flavour. Even using the slower settings of MEDIUM or MED LOW, foods will require much shorter times than conventionally.

The terms we have chosen to designate each power setting should serve only as a guide for choosing the appropriate power level. The recipes in this cookbook will help you decide which setting is best for a particular food. For example we have recommended defrosting foods on MED LOW. Experiment, using your own judgemint and cooking experience as a guide!

WHEN SHOULD YOU USE THE VARIABLE COOKING CONTROL?

HIGH

As the term implies, HIGH is the highest setting and will result in the fastest cooking. HIGH is generally used for:
Fish, Vegetables, Fruits, Hot beverages, some tender meats, bacon, preheating browning dish, melting butter.

MED HIGH

This setting is used primarily for baking or roasting and reheating previously cooked foods. Foods retain more moisture on MED HIGH. Reducing the power to MED means less stirring and watching. Use MED HIGH for:

  to reheat leftovers
  to warm pre-baked bread products (doughnuts, rolls, biscuits)
  to roast chicken or pork
  to cook some casseroles
  to cook foods which contain cheese, cream sauce or sour cream.

MEDIUM

The MEDIUM setting is extremely versatile as you can see from the chart below.
It can be used for some defrosting and roasting, as well as for simmering. Soups and stews are cooked on this setting. Use for:

Braised steak	Chuck steak (boneless)
Rice (uncooked)	Beefburgers
Baked pork chops	Melt cheese
Defrost whole chickens	Baked eggs
Frozen casseroles (Defrost and reheat)	Defrost layer cake

MED LOW

Even the MED LOW setting is more flexible than the name implies. It can be used for cooking less tender cuts of meat for softening cream cheese or butter, and for simmering at an even slower rate than on MEDIUM.

LOW

For keeping foods warm or use to develop the flavour of a sauce.

19

Recipe Conversion

Many conventional recipes can be adapted to microwave cooking with few changes other than a shortened cooking time. Your best guide is a microwave recipe for a similar type of food. Compare the amount and type of main bulky ingredients and liquid. If they are similar, use the container, cooking techniques, power level and time recommended in the microwave recipe to convert your conventional recipe.

Watch the food carefully, and check for doneness after the minimum time. If longer cooking is needed, add more time in small amounts. Be sure to allow standing time for foods which require it.

At the beginning of each microwave section of this book, you'll find directions for microwaving specific foods and suggestions for recipe conversion.

Moist foods, like chicken, seafood, minced beef, vegetables, fruits and saucy main dishes or casseroles convert well. Dry or crusty foods may have a moist surface when microwaved.

Techniques like covering, steaming and stirring, are common to both conventional and microwave cooking. A recipe which calls for these techniques should convert easily and give excellent results when microwaved.

No change in ingredients should be needed for foods which are heated rather than cooked, such as dips, spreads, and some casseroles, or foods which are brought to a boil but not simmered, like white sauce or pudding.

Recipe Conversion (continued)

Conventional | Microwave

Reduce liquid in recipes which call for raw ingredients, simmering, or baking longer than is needed to heat foods through. Little evaporation occurs during microwaving. Use two-thirds the liquid and add more, if needed, as you cook.

Omit fat needed to brown foods and prevent sticking in conventional cooking. A small amount of butter or olive oil may be used for flavour.

Season To Taste

Use less highly flavored seasonings, like garlic, chili, curry powder or sage. After microwaving, correct seasoning to taste. Small amounts of mild herbs and spices need not be changed.

Conventional

Microwave

Cut less tender meat, like stewing beef, and dense vegetables, like potatoes and carrots, in smaller pieces than you would for conventional stews and soups. Small, uniform pieces microwave rapidly and evenly.

HIGH (100%)   Reduced Power

Power level depends on the type of food to be microwaved. To speed cooking, use HIGH (100%) for casseroles which can be stirred, and tender meats, like chicken or minced beef, which are cooked with a sauce of tomatoes, broth or wine. Lower power levels are required for less tender meats, heat-sensitive foods like eggs, cream, cheese, and layered casseroles.

Cooking time depends on the quantity and type of food, so a comparable microwave recipe is your most accurate guide. Microwaving time may be one-quarter to one-third of conventional time. Check for doneness frequently and add more time in small amounts.

Change dish size and time when you change the yield of a microwave recipe. Whether you double a recipe, or cook half of it, level of food should be the same depth as the original microwave recipe. If food is spread too thinly, it will overcook or dry out. It will boil over if dish is too full. To double recipe, double the ingredients, then increase liquid by one-quarter to one-third; increase time by one-half to two-thirds. For half a recipe, use half the ingredients, cut time by one-third.

Top casseroles with bread or crouton crumbs, crushed potato chips, or a mixture of crumbs and Parmesan cheese. Add topping after the final stirring to keep surface crisp.

Substitute quick-cooking rice for raw rice, or canned kidney beans for dried, when these ingredients are combined with foods which would overcook in the time needed to rehydrate dry foods.

Add delicate or quick-cooking ingredients, like seafood and cheese, toward the end of microwaving, to avoid toughening them.

Using the Recipes

All Recipes in this book are written in both metric and imperial measurements. Do not mix the measurements.

Times quoted are approximate. Many factors can affect the cooking time. Initial starting temperature, size of container, shape of container, size of eggs.

Check foods before the completion of cooking. Time can always be added, but not taken away.

If you are doubling the recipe then add half the time again. Do not double up.

If you halve the recipe then the timing should be two thirds of the original time. Not half.

ALL COOKING TIMES ARE APPROXIMATE.

Jelly Cubes

When making a Jelly break up the cubes into a microwave container. Heat for approximately 40 seconds on HIGH. Stir well and gradually stir required water. Then refrigerate till set.

Melting Chocolate

To melt chocolate as a quick topping for cakes, break the chocolate into a glass bowl. Then heat for 1—2 minutes on HIGH. (timing depends on the amount of chocolate). The chocolate will still appear to be in blocks. Stir well until smooth.

Dried Fruit

Save time with dried fruit. Instead of soaking over night. Cover with boiling water and heat on MEDIUM HIGH for 4—5 minutes and allow to stand for an hour before cooking.

Helpful Hints and Tips

Drying Herbs - wash herbs, remove any stalks and then spread herbs onto kitchen paper set on the turntable. Heat on LOW until herbs dry. Timing will depend on type and quantity of herb, so watch them all the time.

Cleaning Jam Jars - to get the last traces of jam out of the jar, remove the lid and heat on HIGH until the jam is liquid. You can then pour out all the jam.

Sterilizing jam jars - when jam or mamalade making, place a small quantity of water in the base of the jar and heat on HIGH until water has boiled for 2—3 mins. Remove water and jars are ready for filling.

Citrus fruit - To get a better yield from your citrus fruit, place into the microwave oven; 1 lemon for about 20 seconds on HIGH. They will also be easier to peel.

Refreshing Biscuits, Bread & Cakes - Put stale cakes, biscuits or bread onto kitchen paper and warm on a MEDIUM setting to refresh. The same can be done with stale cereals or crisps.

Gelatine - place the gelatine and liquid (as per the recipe) in the microwave and heat the water. The gelatine will dissolve when stirred.

Softening butter or cheese - soften butter or cream cheese by heating on LOW for a few seconds. Remember to remove foil wrappings first. Unripe cheeses, such as brie or camembert can be ripened by heating on LOW for a few seconds.

Skinning tomatoes - make a small slit in the tomato and heat on HIGH until just warm. The skins will then come off easily.

Marzipan - soften marzipan so that it is easier to knead. Heat on MEDIUM LOW until soft.

Breadcrumbs - to dry breadcrumbs, place on kitchen paper and heat until dried.

Coffee - left over perculated coffee can be reheated on HIGH.

Breadmaking - warm flour on HIGH for 15 seconds to assest in breadmaking.

CONVECTION COOKING

What is Convection Cooking?

Professional chefs and bakers have used convection ovens for over 3 decades; in recent years, convection ovens have been introduced for use in the home. A convection oven differs from a conventional oven because in most of them the heating element is outside the oven cavity. The entire cavity can be used for cooking.
A high speed fan circulates air past the heat source and around the food. Warm air begins to surround the food as soon as the oven is turned on. A convection oven cooks food with hot air, but because the air is moving, it heats food faster. Excessively hot air does not collect at the top of the oven, and cool air is moved away from the food and reheated.

Convection Cooking

Cooking by Convection will cook foods in a similar way that a conventional oven roasts or bakes. However, when cooking by Convection, the hot air is blown around the oven, which means the oven will heat up quicker than a conventional oven and the heat will be the same temperature throughout. Foods will be evenly browned when baked, because of the convected hot air, and the turntable system; therefore, there is no need to re arrange foods during the cooking. There are two racks supplied with the oven, the high rack allows you to use a shelf arrangement in the oven when cooking more than one item at a time.

When to Use Convection

Use Convection cooking for baking small items, i.e. foods which should be brown and have a crisp finish. The following items are suitable for this system:
Buns, biscuits, scones, pastries, souffles.

How to Cook by Convection

The controls are very easy to use. The temperature is marked in Centigrade. Because of the efficiency of the convection system, reduce the temperature when using your own recipes. When cooking by Convection, foods may be cooked in conventional roasting tins, cake tins, oven to tableware, ovenable board. If cooking one item, place this directly on turntable, close the door, set the timer to the cooking time, and press the start pad. The oven will switch off at the end of the selected cooking time, test the food before removing from the oven if necessary reset the timer for another few minutes. When cooking two items of food both racks may be used. Place the high rack on the turntable which will support one dish, the other may be placed on the turntable immediately under the trivet.

25

Convection Utensils

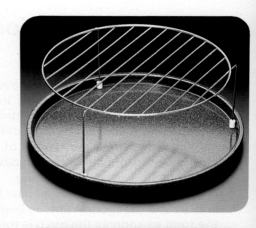

High rack serves as a shelf for two-level cooking, such as layer cakes or biscuits.
Use it for convection and grill cooking, not for microwave alone.

Metal

Oven glass

Glass ceramic

Ovenable paper

Specially designed plastics

DUAL COOKING

To Use Dual Cook. Convection and Microwave

The Dual Cook System enables you to achieve the results your conventional oven gives but cooked in a much shorter time, due to microwaves, results neither one can achieve alone.

Microwaving brings out the natural flavours of food and keeps them moist or juicy, but most foods do not brown. Those which do brown, like joints and turkeys do not have a dry crisp surface. Convection heat browns and crisps food beautifully if cooked by convection alone, breads or cakes may overbrown or develop a thick crust before the inside is done. In the dual oven convection heat seals and browns the outside perfectly while microwave energy makes sure the interior is done.

A Guide to Using Dual Cook

When converting conventional recipes the following principles should be followed:-

1. Cut time by 2/3rd to ½ the normal cooking time given for conventional recipes.

2. Cut the temperature by 10% from conventional recipe temperatures.

3. As a general guide use microwave **MED LOW** on recipes. This can then be adjusted higher or lower if necessary.

4. Cook on the low rack where ever possible.

5. Check dishes a few minutes before the end of cooking time to see if they are cooked.

6. Test cakes in the traditional way by using a skewer to see if the centre is cooked.

Conversion of Recipes for Use on Dual Cooking Programmes

The Sharp Convection microwave cooker offers complete flexibility with its many variable programmes.

Satisfactory results will be achieved everytime, crisp pastries golden in colour, cakes and puddings light in texture and roasts and meat dishes cooked to perfection.

Your oven recipes can be converted by observing the following guide lines.

1. **Preheating of the oven** is unnecessary. The most favourable results will be achieved from a cold start.

2. **Placement of food within the oven.**
   a. For all baked and frozen convenience foods, as well as reheating foods not in foil containers, use of the metal racks provided is recommended.
   b. When cooking roasts or meat portions, the splash guard is used on the turntable. The splash guard will alleviate splashing onto the oven walls. It is useful when making gravy sauce.
   c. For reheating foods in metal containers the low rack is recommended.
   d. Large items like large fruit cakes etc should be positioned directly onto the turntable. Large turkey should be positioned on the splash guard seated on the turntable.

Note

During dual cooking some metal baking utensils may cause arcing when they come in contact with the turntable, oven walls or accessory racks. Arcing is a discharge of electricity that occurs when microwaves come in contact with metal.

If arcing occurs when using a metal utensil, place a heat resistant dish (glass pie plate, glass pizza dish or dinner plate) between the utensil and low rack (on the turntable). If arching still occurs, discontinue the use of that particular utensil.

You should select the cooking mode at DUAL COOK.

Dual Cooking Utensils

A wide variety of utensils may be used in convection and dual cooking. Many of them are also suitable for microwaving alone. Microwave-only paper and plastic products should not be used for dual cooking or placed in the oven while it is still hot from convection cooking.

Be sure to use hot pads when handling utensils. They become hot from convection and dual cooking.

The metal carousel is a utensil itself: a drip pan under the rack during roasting and grilling, or a baking sheet for bread and cookies.

When roasting meat or poultry it is advisable to place the splash guard. This will help to eliminate splashing in the oven.

Metal and aluminum foil tins are safe for dual as well as convection cooking. During the convection cycle heat transferred from the tin cooks the bottom and sides of food. During the microwave cycle, energy penetrates from the top.
If arching occurs when using a metal utensil, place a heat resistant dish (glass pie plate, glass pizza dish or dinner plate) between the pan and low rack (on the turntable).

Oven glass is excellent for convection, dual and microwave cooking. Stoneware and pottery utensils designed for use in ovens may be used if they are also microwave-safe.

Glass ceramic casseroles go from oven to table. They are microwave-safe and heat resistant.

Ovenable paper is designed for use in both microwave and conventional ovens up to 200°C, so it's suitable for convection or dual cooking too. Other paper products used for microwaving alone, such as paper napkins and toweling cannot be used with convection, dual and grill heat.

Special Plastics polyester plastics are heat resistant to temperatures of 200°C to 220°C as well as microwave-safe. They are sold as dual purpose utensils and can be used. Do not use any other plastics for dual and convection cooking.

Roasting Techniques for dual Cooking

Preheating the oven is not necessary for roasted meat and poultry. For moist, tender, perfectly done meat in a fraction of the conventional time, just place the meat in the oven and cook.

Season meat and place splash guard on the turntable, put the low rack on the splash guard.
Put meat on the low rack.
The splash guard catches the drippings.

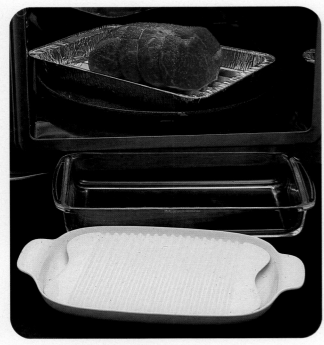

Optional utensils are an oven glass baking dish or 25 cm casserole. Elevate meat on a heat-resistant rack, if desired, and place utensil on carousel.

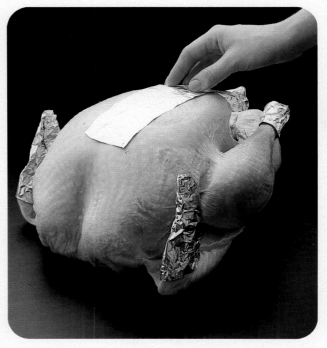

Shield thin or bony areas of roasts or breast, wing tips and legs of birds to prevent overbrowning, especially if meat has been defrosted by microwave. Be sure foil does not touch trivet. Remove shielding from fresh meat after half the time, and from defrosted meat after three-quarter of the time.

Check for required cooking temperature after minimum time using a meat thermometer. If meat is not done cook 5 minutes longer and check again. Leave to stand wrapped in foil for 5 — 10 minutes before carving.

Roast less tender cuts of beef in heat resistant casserole, or cook in a roasting bag set in a baking dish using reduced temperature and power settings.

GRILLING

The Infra-Red Grill system on your Jet Convection oven is both economical and efficient. It heats quickly saving time and energy.

For the initial period, whilst the grill browns and crisps there is also convected hot air in the cavity to speed the cooking of food.

The Infra-Red Grill is safety situated inset into the roof of the oven cavity giving maximum usage of the 1.3 cu.ft oven capacity.

The turntable system ensures even browness with minimum attention.

The Infra-Red Grill has been designed with the aim of achieving maximum safety and efficiency for the user.

It is easy to use and there is no need to preheat before use. The Infra-Red grill is ideal for cooking steaks and chops traditionally, giving succulent results.

It is also ideal to use for browning and crisping many dishes cooked by microwave for traditional results cooked in a fraction of the time.

Grilling Techniques

Set oven for GRILL. Season meat on both sides, if desired. Slash fat at 2.5 cm intervals to prevent curling.
Place splash guard on the turntable, put the high rack on the splash guard and meat on the high rack.

Cook for the minimum time recommended in the chart; then test to see if cooked sufficiently. Time varies with the thickness or weight of meat, and is longer for frozen meat.

GRILL food in advance, if desired, then slice. Individual servings may be reheated as needed by microwaving at MEDIUM (50%).

DEFROSTING

Thawing Frozen Foods

Thawing food, especially meats, with the microwave oven is not only faster than any other method, it can also give better results.

Once frozen meat is thawed, it begins to lose its juices. With a microwave oven, you can thaw meat just before you plan to cook it, for highest juiciness and quality.

Microwave thawing doesn't take a lot of fuss, but some attention is needed to make sure that parts of the meat do not start to cook before the centre is thawed. MEDIUM-LOW is fast enough to be convenient, but gentle enough to give good results. At MEDIUM meat thaws in about one-third less time, but needs more attention.

Place plastic or paper-wrapped package of frozen food directly in oven. To speed thawing, remove wrappings as soon as possible and cover food with plastic wrap to hold in heat. Foil-wrapped foods must be unwrapped.

Start thawing turkey breast side down; shield warm areas and turn over after each quarter of time. Let turkey stand 20 to 30 minutes after thawing, until giblets and neck can be removed and breast meat under wings is completely thawed.

Break up or separate minced beef, cubed meat, chicken pieces, or fish fillets after one-third of thawing time. Remove any thawed pieces. Place remainder in baking dish to complete thawing. Turn over flat roasts, steaks, chops, or chickens after half the time. If the package contains several steaks or chops, separate as soon as possible and place in baking dish.

Turn over large roasts after each quarter of thawing time. As you turn, touch meat for warm areas and shield these with small pieces of foil. Let roast stand 10 minutes after first half of time and 10 to 20 minutes after second half. Thaw meats and poultry only until they can be pierced to the centre with a skewer. Surface or cavity should feel cool but not icy. Cook as soon as possible to prevent loss of juices.

Defrosting Chart for Meat

FOOD	QUANTITY & TIME	VARIABLE CONTROL	METHOD	STANDING TIME
Joint (Beef Pork, Lamb)	450g (1 lb) 8-10 mins	MED LOW	Turn over after half the time. Shield as needed.	45-60 mins
Minced Beef	450g (1 lb) 8 mins	MED LOW	Break apart, remove any thawed pieces as soon as possible. Place remainder in baking dish.	5 mins
Steak 1.87 cm (3/4'') Thick	450g (1 lb) 8 mins	MED LOW	Turn over after half the time. Shield as needed.	5 mins
Chops	450g (1 lb) 8 mins	MED LOW	Separate and turn over once.	5 mins
Liver	450g (1 lb) 8-10 mins	MED LOW	Separate and rearrange once.	5-10 mins
Sausages	450g (1 lb) 6-7 mins	MED LOW	Separate and rearrange once.	10 mins
Bacon	225g (8 oz) 4-5 mins	MED LOW	Separate rashers during defrosting.	5 mins
Beefburgers	¼ pounders 4 4-5 mins	MED LOW	Turn over after half defrosting time.	5-10 mins
Veal Escallopes	450g (1 lb) 7-9 mins	MED LOW	Turn over after half defrosting time.	10-15 mins

Poultry Defrosting Chart

FOOD	QUANTITY & TIME	POWER CONTROL	METHOD	STAND
Whole Chicken	450g (1 lb) 8-9 mins per lb	MED LOW	Breast side down first. Turn over after half the time. Shield as needed.	30-45 mins
Turkey	450g (1 lb) 8-10 mins	MED	Breast side down first. Turn over after half the time. Shield as needed.	45-60 mins
Duck	450g (1 lb) 7-9 mins	MED LOW	Breast side down first. Turn over after half the time. Shield as needed.	30-45 mins
Pheasant	450g (1 lb) 6-8 mins	MED LOW	Breast side down first. Turn over after half the time. Shield if necessary.	20-30 mins
Chicken Drumsticks	450g (1 lb) 6-8 mins	MED LOW	Turn over halfway through defrosting.	10-15 mins
Chicken Portions (Bone in)	450g (1 lb) 7-8 mins	MED LOW	Turn over halfway through defrosting.	10-15 mins
Chicken Breasts (Boneless)	450g (1 lb) 6-7 mins	MED LOW	Turn over halfway through defrosting.	10-15 mins

Reheating

Foods reheated in the microwave oven taste freshly cooked, not reheated. Suit the power level to the food. A bowl of leftover vegetables can be reheated at HIGH (100%), while lasagna, which contains sensitive cheese and cannot be stirred, should be reheated at MEDIUM (50%).

Casseroles. Cover dish tightly. Stir several times during cooking, especially if casserole has been refrigerated. If casserole cannot be stirred, reheat at MEDIUM (50%).

Meats. Medium to thin slices reheat best. Cover meat with sauce, gravy or paper towel. Top with plastic wrap to hold in heat. Microwave at MED-IUM (50%) about 45 seconds to 1 minute per serving.

Reheating (continued)

Plates of food. Arrange food with thickest parts of meat and bulky vegetables to outside of plate. Place quick-to-heat foods in centre. Spread single serving of a main dish in even layer on plate. Cover with plastic wrap. Reheat until underside of plate feels warm in the centre.

Vegetables. Wrap large, whole vegetable in plastic wrap. Cover dishes of vegetables tightly and stir during cooking, if possible.

Pie. Place whole pie in glass pie dish or slice of pie on serving plate. Reheat whole pie at MEDIUM-HIGH (70%) 5 to 7 minutes, and one slice 30 seconds at HIGH (100%).

RE-HEATING

Before re-heating food in your microwave oven always remove food from metal dish or tin and put into suitable microwave container.

ITEMS	QUANTITIES		POWER	TIME	METHOD
Baked Beans	175 g	7 oz approx	HIGH	2–2½ mins	Covered
	375 g	15 oz	HIGH	3½–4 mins	Covered
Tinned Tomatoes	375 g	15 oz	HIGH	3–3½ mins	Covered
Cream of Thick Soup	175 g	7 oz	HIGH	2–2½ mins	Covered
	600 ml	1 pt.	HIGH	3½–4 mins	Covered
Thin Soup	175 g	7 oz	HIGH	1½–2 mins	Covered
	600 ml	1 pt.	HIGH	3–3½ mins	Covered
Tinned Peas	250 g	10 oz	HIGH	2 mins	Covered
Tinned Sweetcorn	250 g	10 oz	HIGH	1½–2 mins	Covered
Tinned Carrots	250 g	10 oz	HIGH	1½–2 mins	Covered
Tinned New Potatoes	250 g	10 oz	HIGH	2–2½ mins	Covered
Marrowfat Peas	250 g	10 oz	HIGH	2–2½ mins	Covered
Tinned Macaroni Cheese	175 g	7 oz	HIGH	1½–2 mins	Covered
	375 g	15 oz	HIGH	3–3½ mins	Covered
Tinned Rice Pudding	375 g	15 oz	HIGH	2½–3½ mins	Covered
Tinned Sponge Pudding	Heinz		HIGH	1½–2 mins	Covered
Meat (frozen)	1 serving		MED HIGH	1–2 mins	Cover loosely
Chicken Portions,					
Chops, Hamburgers,	2 servings		MED HIGH	2½–4½ mins	Cover loosely
Meat Loaf Slices					
Meat Slices (frozen)	1 or more servings		MEDIUM	1–3 mins/serving	Cover with gravy or plastic wrap. Check after 30 sec./serving.
Beef, Ham, Pork, Turkey					
Meat Slices (fresh)	1 or more servings		MEDIUM	¾–1 min/serving	Cover with gravy or plastic wrap. Check after 30 sec./serving
Beef, Ham, Pork, Turkey					
Chicken	200 g	8 oz	HIGH	1½–2½ mins	Covered
Casserole	For 4 people		MED HIGH	10–14 mins	Stir twice during heating
	Single portion		MED HIGH	2–3 mins	Stir once during heating
Fresh Vegetables	100 g	4 oz	HIGH	30 secs–1 min	Covered
	450 g	1 lb	HIGH	2–2½ mins	Covered
Frozen Vegetables	125 g	5 oz	HIGH	¾–1½ mins	Cover.
	250 g	1 oz	HIGH	1½–2½ mins	Stir after half the time.

RE-HEATING

Before re-heating food in your microwave oven always remove food from metal dish or tin and put into suitable microwave container.

ITEMS	QUANTITIES		POWER	TIME	METHOD
Sponge Pudding	4 servings		HIGH	$1\frac{1}{2}$—2 mins	Covered
Christmas Pudding	Mini Pudding		HIGH	1—$1\frac{1}{4}$ mins	Covered
	600 g	$1\frac{1}{2}$ lb	HIGH	3—$3\frac{1}{2}$ mins	Covered
Fruit Crumble	4 servings		HIGH	3—$3\frac{1}{2}$ mins	Covered
Custard	1 pt.	600 ml	HIGH	3—$3\frac{1}{2}$ mins	
	$\frac{1}{2}$ pt	300 ml	HIGH	$1\frac{1}{2}$—2 mins	
Sausages	200 g	8 oz	HIGH	$1\frac{1}{2}$—2 mins	Cover with kitchen paper
Plated meal of meat & vegetables	Average servings		HIGH	$2\frac{1}{2}$—4 mins	
Rolls	1 roll		HIGH	8—12 sec.	Wrap single rolls in paper towel. For serveral rolls, line plate with paper towel; cover rolls with another towel.
Dinner or Breakfast	2 rolls			11—15 sec.	
	4 rolls			18—22 sec.	
Pie (frozen)	whole		MED HIGH	5—7 mins	
	1 slice		HIGH	30 sec.	
Mince Pies	1		HIGH	15 sec.	Place on kitchen paper
(cooked)	4		HIGH	1 mins	

ALL THESE TIMES ARE APPROXIMATE AND WILL DEPEND ON STARTING TEMPERATURE CONTAINER AND PORTION SIZE.

Convenience Foods

With a microwave oven, convenience foods can be ready to serve in far less time than it takes conventionally. Most heat-and-eat convenience foods provide microwaving instructions on the packages. These instructions are usually for HIGH (100%), which is on all microwave ovens.

Microwave can also shorten the time needed for foods which are usually thawed several hours at room temperature. MEDIUM-LOW (30%) is gentle enough to thaw cakes and cream pies without melting the delicate frostings or fillings. Let these foods stand to complete thawing.

TV Dinners. Remove lid from foil pan. Return tray to box and place in centre of turntable. Microwave at HIGH (100%) until heated through.

Frosted Cakes. Place cake on serving plate. Microwave at MEDIUM-LOW (30%), until a wooden pick inserted in centre of cake meets little resistance. Watch closely; if frosting starts to soften, remove cake from oven. Let cake stand 15 to 25 minutes.

Cream Pies. Remove pie from foil dish to pie dish or serving plate. Microwave at MEDIUM-LOW (30%) until a wooden pick inserted in centre of filling meets no resistance. Let pie stand 5 minutes before serving.

Convenience Foods

FOOD	QUANTITY	METHOD	DEFROSTING TIME ON MED LOW	SETTING & TIME	COMMENTS
Meat-Reheat					
Individual Meat Pie (precooked)	1	Remove foil dish. Stand on kitchen paper.	3 mins. Stand 1 min.	HIGH — ¾-1½ mins.	Stand 2 mins.
Family Meat Pie (precooked)	450g (1 lb)	Remove foil dish. Stand on kitchen paper.	8 mins. Stand 4 mins. 4 mins.	MED HIGH — 5 mins.	Stand 4 mins. halfway through
Cornish Pasty (precooked)	1	Stand on kitchen paper.		HIGH — ¾ min.	Stand 2 mins.
Sausage Roll (precooked)	1	Stand on kitchen paper.		HIGH — 15-30 secs.	Stand 1 min.
Meat Casserole	100g (4 oz)	Place in dish & cover.	4 mins. Stand 3 mins. 2 mins.	HIGH — 5 mins.	Stir halfway through cooking
	225g (8 oz)		6 mins. Stand 4 mins. 3 mins.	HIGH — 7 mins.	
Lasagne	Individual	Remove foil dish, place on plate. Cover.	5 mins. Stand 4 mins. 3 mins.	MED HIGH — 4 mins.	Stand 3 mins. before serving
	Family size	Remove foil dish, place in serving dish. Cover.	8 mins. Stand 6 mins. 4 mins.	MED HIGH — 9 mins.	Stand 5 mins. before serving
Frozen Meats					
Indiv. Boil in Bag meals	225g (8 oz)	Puncture bag. Place on plate.	6 mins. Stand 3 mins.	HIGH — 2½- 3 mins.	Stand 2 mins.
Shepherds Pie	450g (1 lb)	Remove foil, place on serving dish.	10 mins.	MED HIGH — 5-6 mins.	Stand 5 mins.
Beefburgers	1 2 4	Place on kitchen paper.	Cook from frozen	HIGH — 2 mins. 4 mins. 6 mins.	Turn over once during cooking
Roast Meat in Gravy	100g (4 oz)	Remove foil, place on plate.	4-5 mins.	HIGH — 2 mins.	Separate slices after defrosting
Lasagne/Moussaka	450g (1 lb)	Remove foil, place on dish, cover.	8 mins. Stand 6 mins. 4 mins.	MED HIGH — 9 mins.	Stand 5 mins. before serving
Sausage Rolls (precooked)	1	Place on kitchen paper.	½- 1 min. Stand 1 min.	HIGH — 15-30 sec.	Stand for 1 min.
	2		1 -1½ min. Stand 1 min.	HIGH — 30-45 sec.	Stand 1 min.
	4		1½ -2 min. Stand 1 min.	HIGH — 1 -1½ min.	Stand 2 mins.
Plate dinner for 1	Meat potato and 2 Veg.	Place on plate, cover with cling film.	7-8 mins. Stand 4 mins.	MED HIGH — 3-4 mins.	Stand 2-3 mins.
Fish					
Kippers	1	Place in greaseproof paper.		HIGH — 3 mins.	
2 cod steaks	225g (8 oz)	Place on plate.	6 mins. Stand 4 mins.	HIGH — 3 mins.	Turn over half-way through defrosting
Boil-in-Bag- smoked haddock	175g (6 oz)	Puncture bag. Place on plate.	6 mins. Stand 4 mins.	HIGH — 4 mins.	Separate fillets after defrosting

* Care must be taken when heating foods with a high sugar/fat content, heating times are exceptionally short.
(Timings given are to be used as a guide to reheating times.)

Convenience Foods (Cont.)

FOOD	QUANTITY	METHOD	DEFROSTING TIME ON MED LOW	SETTING & TIME	COMMENTS
Fish (Cont.)					
Fish steak in Sauce-Boil in Bag	175g (6 oz)	Puncture bag. Place on plate.	5 mins. Stand 4 mins.	HIGH — 3 mins.	Stand 4 mins.
Fish Fingers	2	Place on Plate.	1½ mins.	HIGH — 1½ mins.	Dot with butter
	4	Arrange in circle on plate.	2½ mins.	HIGH — 2½ mins.	before cooking
Fish Cakes	2 (each 50g (2 oz))	Place on plate.	4 mins.	HIGH — 1½ mins.	Dot with butter before cooking
Trout (frozen)	175g (6 oz)	Place on plate. Cover.	Cook from frozen	HIGH — 4½ mins.	Season with lemon juice, & black pepper before cooking
Bread					
Large white sliced	1	Place on kitchen paper.	7 — 9 mins.		Stand 10 mins.
Small loaf	1	Place on kitchen paper.	4 — 5 mins.		Stand 5 mins.
Roll	1	Place on kitchen paper.		HIGH — 15 sec.	
Pizza (frozen)	Individual	Remove wrapping.	Cook from frozen	HIGH — 2 mins.	Stand 1 min.
	1 large	Place on cooking rack or kitchen paper.		HIGH — 4-5 mins.	Stand 3 mins.
Puddings & Cakes					
Indiv. Fruit Pie	1	Remove foil dish. Place on plate.	1½ mins. Stand 2 mins.	HIGH — 1 min.	
Cheesecake with Fruit topping	1 slice	Remove foil dish. Place on plate.	1½ mins.		Stand 10 mins.
	1 family sized	Place on plate.	4 mins.		Stand 30 mins.
Jam doughnut	1	Place on kitchen paper.	1 min.		
Cream Sponge	275g (10 oz)	Place on serving plate.	1-1½ mins.		Stand until cream thawed
Miscellaneous					
Chocolate	100g (4 oz)	Break into squares.		HIGH — 2½-3 mins.	Stir well
Jelly	135g (4¾ oz)	Break in cubes place in jug, add 150ml (¼ pt) water.		HIGH — 2 mins.	Add remaining water, Stir well
Butter/marg. frozen	225g (8 oz)	Remove foil wrapping. Place on dish.	30-45 sec. Stand 1 min, 30 sec. Stand 1 min.		
Puff & Shortcrust Pastry	215g (7½ oz)	Remove any foil wrapping.	2 mins.		Stand 5 mins.
	375g (13 oz)	Place on plate.	3 mins.		Stand 5 mins.
Bacon	2 rashers	Place on rack or kitchen paper.		HIGH — 1-1½ mins.	Cover with kitchen paper to stop splashing
Quick Porridge Oats	1 cup oats	Combine oats & water in a large bowl.		HIGH — 6 mins.	Stir well

* Certain foods, require 3 sequences defrost/standing time followed by defrost again,
  eg *Family meat pie 8 mins. stand
                            4 mins. 4 mins.
  This would be 8 mins defrost, standing time 4 mins followed by further 4 mins defrost.
* Care must be taken when heating foods with a high sugar/fat content, heating times are exceptionally short.
  (Timings given are to be used as a guide to reheating times.)

COOKING CHART

Meat Roasting Chart

FOOD	TIME (in mins) per 450g (1 lb)	SETTING	MODE
Rib of Beef			
Rare	9—14	MED 160°C	DUAL COOK
Medium	11—16	MED 160°C	DUAL COOK
Welldone	13—18	MED 160°C	DUAL COOK
Beef Silverside/ Topside			
Rare	10—13	MED 160°C	DUAL COOK
Medium	12—17	MED 160°C	DUAL COOK
Welldone	14—19	MED 160°C	DUAL COOK
Brisket of Beef	30—35	MED LOW 130°C	DUAL COOK
Lamb leg or fillet			
Medium	12—17	MED 160°C	DUAL COOK
Welldone	14—19	MED 160°C	DUAL COOK
Lamb shoulder			
Welldone	14—19	MED 160°C	DUAL COOK
Pork			
Rolled Shoulder (boneless/with bone)	10—15	MED 230°C	DUAL COOK
Boneless leg	10—15	MED 230°C	DUAL COOK
Leg Bone in	11—16	MED 230°C	DUAL COOK
Gammon Joint	14—19	MED 180°C	DUAL COOK

GENERAL PROCEDURE:

Season as desired.

Place meat on Low Rack, and set on Turntable with Splash Guard.

Turn over 2—3 times during cooking.

After cooking stand for 10—15 mins.

Poultry Roasting Chart

FOOD	TIME (in mins) per 450g (1 lb)	SETTING		MODE
Chicken (whole)	8—13	MED HIGH	200°C	DUAL COOK
Turkey	3—8	MED HIGH	200°C	DUAL COOK
Duck whole	5—10	MED	180°C	DUAL COOK
Pheasant	6—11	MED	180°C	DUAL COOK
Chicken portions	7—11	MED HIGH	200°C	DUAL COOK
Duck portions	6—10	MED	180°C	DUAL COOK

GENERAL PROCEDURE:

Season as desired.

Place meat on Low Rack, and set on Turntable with Splash Guard.

Turn over 2—3 times during cooking.

After cooking stand for 10—15 mins.

Grilling Chart

FOOD	COOKING TIME (in mins)	
	SIDE 1	SIDE 2
*Rump steak		
Rare	4—6	2—3
Medium	5—7	3—5
Welldone	8—11	6—9
Chicken pieces		
0.2 kg (½ lb)	11—12	7—8
1 kg (2 lb)	16—17	11—12
2 kg (4½ lb)	21—22	17—18
Chicken fillet (Boneless breast)		
0.2 kg (½ lb)	8—9	4—5
1 kg (2 lb)	13—14	8—9
2 kg (4½ lb)	18—19	14—15
Pork chops	8—9	6—7
Lamb chops loin	7—8	5—6
Lamb liver	6—7	3—4
Gammon steaks	7—8	6—7
Bacon	3—5	2—4
Sausage		
Thin link	6—7	3—4
Thick link	6—7	4—5
Trout	7—8	5—6
Toast	4—5	2—3
Cheese on Toast	4—5	3—4
Gratin (Macaroni)	6—8	

N.B.
The grilling time is versatile for different amount of the foods.
Use this as a guideline and add or reduce the time depending on the amount of foods.
*Steak grilling times will vary according to the thickness of the steak, the times should be used as a guide minimum time for thin steak maximum time for thick steak.

GENERAL PROCEDURE:
    Season as desired.
    Place food on High Rack and set on Turntable.
    (If cooking meat, use Splash Guard.)
    Turn over after grilling SIDE 1, then continue grilling SIDE 2.
    When grilling gratin, line a pyrex or china gratin dish approx. 3 cm height.
    And place on High Rack. Grill for required time.

Fish Cooking Chart

FOOD	AMOUNT & TIME	SETTING	METHOD	STANDING TIME
Fish fillets	450g (1 lb) 4-5 mins per (1 lb)	HIGH	Place in non-metallic dish cover.	2-3 mins
Cod or Haddock Steaks	450g (1 lb) 5-6 mins per (1 lb)	HIGH	Cover dish while cooking.	3-4 mins
Lemon sole fillets	225g (8 oz) $2\frac{1}{2}$-3 mins per (1 lb)	HIGH	Cover dish while cooking.	2-3 mins
Dover Sole	450g (1 lb) 4-5 mins per (1 lb)	HIGH	Turn oven half way through cooking.	2-3 mins
Whole Mackerel	450g (1 lb) 5-6 mins per (1 lb)	HIGH	Turn over half way through cooking.	3-4 mins
Trout whole	450g (1 lb) 5-6 mins per (1 lb)	HIGH	Turn over half way through cooking.	3-4 mins
Salmon steaks	450g (1 lb) 5-6 mins per (1 lb)	HIGH	Turn over half way through cooking.	3-4 mins
Whole Salmon	450g (1 lb) 4-5 mins per (1 lb)	HIGH	Cook in $\frac{1}{4}$ pt of boiling liquid.	10-15 mins

Vegetables

Use minimum of water. Some vegetables cook in their own natural moisture. Two tablespoons to 2 ½ fl oz of liquid is usually sufficient for others. Salt after cooking or dissolve salt in water before adding vegetables. Salting vegetables directly dries them out.

Cover dish tightly to hold in steam. Vegetables with skins like potatoes should be pricked with a fork to allow excess steam to escape. Wrap large vegetables without skins in plastic wrap or microwave in a covered casserole.

Quantity and size affect cooking time. Two servings take less time than four; small pieces cook faster than large ones. For fast, even microwaving, cut vegetables in small, uniform pieces and stir once during cooking.

Arrange halved or whole vegetables, like potatoes, in a ring, leaving center open and space between, when possible. Place tender ends of asparagus or broccoli toward centre of dish, so stalks will receive more energy.

Standing time is important, especially with large, whole vegetables. It allows the centre of the vegetable to tenderize without overcooking the outside. During standing, keep the food covered to hold in heat. Long standing times can be used to microwave other foods.

Blanch 1 lb fresh vegetables for the freezer in a covered dish, using 10 fl oz water. Microwave at HIGH (100%) for about the same time recommended for cooking the frozen vegetables in the chart, or until vegetables become hot and begin to change colour. Then immerse vegetables in ice water to stop cooking and cool quickly.

Spread on paper toweling and blot up excess moisture. Package in freezer boxes or heavy plastic bags. Seal tightly, label and freeze. To loose-pack, spread vegetables on cooking sheet and freeze before sealing pieces in large packages.

Fresh Vegetable Chart

VEGETABLE	AMOUNT	COOKING PROCEDURE	COOKING TIME ON HIGH	STANDING TIME
Artichokes Globe	2 medium	Add 75 ml (1/8 pt) water adn 1 x 5 ml tsp. Salt.	5½—8½ mins.	3 mins.
Asparagus	350 g (12 oz)	Add 75 ml (1/8 pt) water. Stir after 3 mins.	4—5 mins.	3 mins.
Beans Broad	450 g (1 lb) shelled	Add 150 ml (1/4 pt) water. Stir after 4 mins.	9—10 mins.	3 mins.
Beans Green	450 g (1 lb)	Add 150 ml (1/4 pt) water. Stir after 4 mins.	9—10 mins.	3 mins.
Broccoli*	225 g (8 oz)	Remove tough part of stalk, split tender ends. Add 3 x 15 ml tbsp water.	5—6 mins.	3 mins.
Brussel Sprouts	225 g (8 oz)	Add 1½ x 15 ml tbsp water. Stir after 3 mins.	8—9 mins.	3 mins.
Cabbage	1 medium	Wash, remove outer leaves, quarter and chop. Add 1½ x 15 ml tbsp water.	10—13 mins.	2 mins.
Carrots	225 g (8 oz)	Peel, slice. Add 1½ x 15 ml tbsp water.	6—7 mins.	3 mins.
Cauliflower*	225 g (8 oz)	Cut into florets. Add 2 x 15 ml tbsp water.	10—12 mins.	3 mins.
Celery	450 g (1 lb)	Add 75 ml (1/8 pt) water.	9—10 mins.	3 mins.
Corn on the Cob	2 ears	Peel back husks, remove silk, leave husks intact or wrap in greaseproof paper. Brush ears with melted butter.	7—10 mins	5 mins.
	4 ears		12—16 mins.	5 mins.
Courgettes	2 medium	Cut into thin slices. Add 25 g (1 oz) butter. Stir after 4 mins.	8—9 mins.	3 mins.
Leeks	225 g (8 oz)	Slice. Add 25 g (1 oz) butter.	3—4 mins.	2 mins.
Mushrooms	225 g (8 oz)	Add 25 g (1 oz) butter.	4—5 mins.	2 mins.
Onions	2 large	Slice. Add 75 ml (1/8 pt) water.	5—6 mins.	3 mins.
Parsnips	4 medium	Dice. Add 75 ml (1/8 pt) water.	8—10 mins.	3 mins.
Peas	450 g (1 lb)	Shell. Add 1½ x 15 ml tbsp water. Stir after 3 mins.	8—9 mins.	3 mins.
Potatoes Baked	1 medium	Pierce skin, wrap in paper towel.	4—5 mins.	4 mins.
	2 medium	Pierce skin, wrap in paper towel.	7—9 mins.	5—10 mins.
	4 medium	Pierce skin, wrap in paper towel.	11—13 mins.	5—10 mins.
Boiled	225 g (8 oz).	Peel, cut into quarters. Add 2 x 15 ml tbsp water.	5—6 mins.	3 mins.
New	225 g (8 oz)	Scrape. Add 2 x 15 ml tbsp water.	5—6 mins.	3 mins.
Spinach	450 g (1 lb)	Wash, remove thick stems. Wrap in cling film	7—8 mins.	2 mins.
Spring Greens	225 g (8 oz)	Wash and shred leaves, wrap in cling film	15 mins.	2 mins.
Swede	225 g (8 oz)	Peel, dice. Add 2 x 15 ml tbsp water.	4—5 mins.	3 mins.
Tomatoes	4 large	Clean, peel, halve. Add 1½ x 15 ml tbsp water.	2—4 mins.	2 mins.
Turnips	225 g (8 oz)	Wash, peel, dice. Add 75 ml (1/8 pt) water. Stir after 5 mins.	4—5 mins.	3 mins.

* Broccoli and whole cauliflower give excellent results on MEDIUM HIGH due to their density.

Broccoli 450 g (1 lb)	9—10 mins. on MEDIUM HIGH
Whole cauliflower	12—15 mins. on MEDIUM HIGH

All vegetables should be cooked in a covered dish.

Frozen Vegetable Cooking Chart

VEGETABLE	AMOUNT	COOKING PROCEDURE	COOKING TIME ON HIGH	STANDING TIME
Beans, Green, cut	225 g (8 oz)	Place in dish. Add 2 x 15 ml tbsp hot water. Cover. Stir after 4 min.	6—7 mins.	3 mins.
Broccoli	225 g (8 oz)	Place in dish. Cover. Stir after 3 min.	$5^1/_2$—$6^1/_2$ mins.	3 mins.
Brussel Sprouts	225 g (8 oz)	Place in dish. Cover. Stir after 3 mins.	4—5 mins.	2 mins.
Carrots	225 g (8 oz)	Place in dish. Cover. Stir after 3 mins.	5—7 mins.	3 mins.
Cauliflower florets	275 g (10 oz)	Place in dish. Add 2 x 15 ml tbsp water. Cover Stir after 3 min.	5—6 mins.	3 mins.
Corn on the cob	1 ear	Place in dish and cover.	4—5 mins.	4 mins.
	2 ears	Place in dish and cover.	7—10 mins.	5 mins.
Peas	225 g (8 oz)	Place in dish and cover.	5—6 mins.	3 mins.
Sweetcorn	225 g (8 oz)	Place in dish and cover.	6 mins.	2 mins.
Vegetable, mixed	225 g (8 oz)	Place in dish and cover.	6 mins.	2 mins.
Oven Chips	100 g (4 oz)	Spread out onto kitchen paper.	$3^1/_2$—4 mins.	2 mins.
	225 g (8 oz)	Spread out onto kitchen paper.	$5^1/_2$—6 mins.	3 mins.

Conversion Charts
(Approximate)

Oven Temperatures

°F	°C	Gas Mark
225	110	¼
250	130	½
275	140	1
300	150	2
325	170	3
350	180	4
375	190	5
400	200	6
425	220	7
450	230	8

Liquid Equivalents

1 fl oz	30 millilitres
¼ pt	150 millilitres
½ pt	300 millilitres
¾ pt	445 millilitres
1 pt	600 millilitres
1¾ pt approx. 1 litre	

Weight

Metric gms	Imperial oz
25g	1 oz
50g	2 ozs
100g	4 ozs
175g	6 ozs
225g	8 ozs
350g	12 ozs
450g	16 ozs

RECIPES

Soups and Starters

Recipe Conversion to Microwave Cooking

SOUPS

When converting soup recipes, reduce the amount of liquid by one-fourth, since there will be less evaporation. Exceptions are soups made with dried beans, peas or lentils, which absorb moisture as they cook.
Reduce salt and other seasonings by one-half. Add more to taste after microwaving.

Type of liquid and main bulky ingredients determines the power level. When making soup with less tender meat, start it at HIGH, then reduce the power to MEDIUM. Vegetable soup and soup with tender meat, like chicken, can be microwaved at HIGH.

Microwaving time is based on quantity; more food takes more time. Your best guide is a microwave recipe for a similar type and quantity of soup.

Cut meat and dense vegetables like carrots and potatoes in thin slices or small cubes for fast, uniform cooking.
HIGH is used for liquid like water, or stock. Milkbased soups which are stirred during cooking can also be microwaved at HIGH, but should be placed in a deep container to prevent boiling over.
MEDIUM-HIGH and MEDIUM are needed for cream, which curdles at HIGH temperatures, and soups which require simmering to develop flavour or tenderize ingredients like stewing beef, uncooked pasta, dried beans or peas.

STARTERS

Recipes for dips, spreads and canapés which are heated, rather than cooked, need no change in ingredients. Mix them in a microwave-safe serving dish and heat, using one of these recipes as a guide to microwaving time and power level.

For bacon-wrapped appetizers, use raw bacon to wrap raw fillings. With cooked or canned fillings, microwave bacon for half its cooking time bafore assembling the appetizers. At serving time, microwave either type of appetizer until the bacon is crisp and brown.

Cheese Fondue

1 clove of garlic
450 g (1 lb) Edam cheese
25 g (1 oz) plain flour
¼ x 5 ml tsp salt
¼ x 5 ml tsp ground nutmeg
⅛ x 5 ml tsp pepper
400 ml (¾ pt) white wine
French bread, cut into 2.5 cm (1'') cubes

1. Rub inside of large casserole with garlic clove-discard.

2. Grate cheese and combine with flour and seasonings in a plastic bag. Shake to coat cheese. Set aside.

3. Pour wine into the casserole. Cook on MEDIUM HIGH until the wine is very hot but not boiling. 2—4 mins. Add all remaining ingredients from plastic bag. Blend with whisk.

4. Cook on MEDIUM HIGH until bubbling 7—9 mins. Stir until smooth.

5. Serve with french bread cubes.

Stuffed Courgettes

3 courgettes
1 x 200 g (7 oz) tin tomatoes - chopped
1 clove of garlic - chopped
75 g (3 oz) peeled prawns
Salt and pepper

Cheese Sauce

25 g (1 oz) plain flour
25 g (1 oz) margarine
300 ml (½ pt) milk
50 g (2 oz) cheddar cheese

1. Slice courgettes in half lengthways and place them into a large dish. Cover with plastic wrap and cook for 3 mins on HIGH until soft.

2. Scoop out the courgette flesh, chop, and mix with remaining filling ingredients. Spoon filling into courgette skins.

3. Prepare cheese sauce. Melt margarine on HIGH for 30 seconds, stir in the flour and blend in the milk. Cook for 3 mins on HIGH until thickened.

4. Whisk the sauce until smooth and stir in the cheese, whisk until cheese is melted.

5. Pour cheese sauce over the courgettes and grill until brown 6—8 mins.

Liver Pâté

225 g (8 oz) chicken livers
1 medium onion - chopped
1 clove garlic - crushed
1 x 15 ml tbsp brandy
2 x 15 ml tbsp double cream
1 egg yolk
Seasoning

Hot Seafood Salad

1 x 200 g (7 oz) tin of tuna fish
1 x 100 g (4 oz) tin of crab meat
100 g (4 oz) peeled prawns
2 tomatoes - chopped
2 spring onions - chopped
2 x 15 ml tbsp prawn salad dressing
1 lettuce - shredded

1. Mix all ingredients together except the lettuce in a large bowl.

2. Heat on HIGH for 2 mins.

3. Place lettuce into four dishes and serve the seafood mixture on top.

Smoked Mackerel Pâté

225 g (8 oz) smoked mackerel - prepared
1 small onion - chopped
12½ g (½ oz) butter
Ground black pepper and salt
1 x 15 ml tbsp chopped parsley
100 ml (4 fl oz) natural yoghurt

1. Cook onion and butter for 3 mins on HIGH.

2. Place fish and all remaining ingredients into a liquidiser or processor and blend well.

3. Spoon into 4 individual ramekin dishes and chill.

1. Place chicken livers, onion, garlic and seasoning in a bowl and cook on HIGH for 3 mins.

2. Liquidise the cooked mixture, add remaining ingredients and blend again.

3. Pour into a dish and chill for 2—3 hours.

Mushrooms à La Grèc

225 g (8 oz) onion - chopped
25 g (1 oz) butter
2 cloves of garlic, finely chopped
225 g (8 oz) mushrooms - sliced
1 x 200 g (7 oz) tin of tomatoes - drained and chopped
1 x 15 ml tbsp tomato puree
¼ x 5 ml tsp black pepper
Salt
¼ x 5 ml tsp celery salt

1. Place onion, butter and garlic into a bowl and microwave on HIGH for 3½ mins.

2. Add remaining ingredients and microwave on HIGH for 2 mins.

Garlic Mushrooms

450 g (1 lb) mushrooms
25 g (1 oz) butter
2 cloves of garlic - crushed
150 ml (¼ pt) double cream
2 x 15 ml tbsp white wine

1. Melt butter on HIGH for 30 seconds, add the garlic and mushrooms and saute for 5 mins on HIGH.

2. Remove mushrooms, add wine and bring to boil for 5 mins on HIGH to reduce liquid. Stir in the cream.

3. Return mushrooms to cream mixture and heat 1½—2 mins on HIGH.

4. Serve in 4 ramekin dishes.

Prawn and Bacon Rolls

225 g (8 oz) prawns
2 x 15 ml tbsp soy sauce
¼ x 5 ml tsp ground ginger
Pinch garlic powder
6 slices bacon each cut into thirds

1. Combine soy sauce, ginger and garlic powder in a small bowl. Add prawns, let stand for 1—2 hours.

2. Wrap a piece of bacon around 2 prawns. Secure with wooden pick. Line carousel turntable with several layers of paper towelling.

3. Arrange appetizers around outer edge of turntable. Microwave on HIGH until bacon is browned about 4—5 mins.

Stuffed Tomatoes

4 large tomatoes (about 775 g (1½ lb))
50 g (2 oz) cooked yellow rice
25 g (1 oz) chopped cooked ham
25 g (1 oz) chopped spring onion
2 x 15 ml tbsp double cream
1 x 5 ml tsp oregano

1. Slice the top off each tomato and set aside. Scoop out the centres of tomatoes and chop.

2. Mix all ingredients together with the flesh of tomatoes.

3. Fill each tomato with the filling and replace the tops.

4. Place the tomatoes on a dish. Cook on MEDIUM HIGH for 1½—2 mins.

French Onion Soup

350 g (¾ lb) onion-thinly sliced
1200 ml (2 pt) hot beef stock (using 3 cubes)
25 g (1 oz) butter
2 x 15 ml tbsp worcester sauce
Salt and pepper

1. Place onions, butter and 1 pint of stock into casserole. Microwave on HIGH for 15 mins.

2. Stir in remaining stock and worcester sauce and season on taste.

3. Heat on HIGH for 4—5 mins. Stand before serving.

Minestrone Soup

1 Medium onion - peeled and chopped
1 Medium leek - chopped
100 g (4 oz) smoked streaky bacon - chopped
25 g (1 oz) margarine
1 medium carrot - chopped
100 g (4 oz) swede - chopped
400 g (14 oz) tin tomatoes - chopped
50 g (2 oz) quick cook macaroni
900 ml (1½ pt) boiling beef stock
¼ x 5 ml tsp ground black pepper
½ x 5 ml tsp salt
½ x 5 ml tsp oregano

1. Sauté the onion, margarine, leek and bacon together on HIGH for 5 mins in a large bowl.

2. Add all other ingredients with the stock and stir.

3. Cook on HIGH for 5 mins then 23—26 mins on MEDIUM.
Allow to stand for 10 mins.

Cream of Tomato Soup

1 medium onion chopped
25 g (1 oz) margarine
50 g (2 oz) smoked bacon chopped
2 x 397 g (14 oz) tin of tomatoes chopped
300 ml (½ pt) chicken stock
150 ml (¼ pt) milk
150 ml (¼ pt) single cream
Seasoning

1. In a large bowl heat the margarine for 30 seconds on HIGH. Add the onion and bacon and cook for 3 mins on HIGH.

2. Add the tomatoes and cook on HIGH for 5—6 mins.

3. Puree the mixture through a sieve or use a blender or food processor.

4. Return the soup to a large bowl adding the stock, milk and cream. Heat on MEDIUM HIGH for 5—6 mins. Do not allow to boil. Stand for 5 mins and serve.

Cream of Celery Soup

350 g (¾ lb) celery
12 g (½ oz) butter
Salt and pepper
450 ml (¾ pt) chicken stock
300 ml (½ pt) milk

1. Place celery and butter in bowl and microwave on HIGH for 5 mins.

2. Add stock and microwave for 10 mins on HIGH.

3. Liquidise until smooth.

4. Add milk and seasoning.

5. Return to bowl and heat 2 mins on HIGH.

Country Farmhouse Vegetable Soup

1 leek - sliced
175 g (6 oz) parsnip - diced
175 g (6 oz) carrot - sliced finely
175 g (6 oz) potato - diced
3 rashers of streaky bacon - chopped
1200 ml (2 pint) of beef stock
2 x 15 ml tbsp cornflour
4 x 15 ml tbsp water
Salt and pepper

1. Chop bacon and microwave on HIGH for 2 mins.

2. Place all vegetables and stock into casserole and microwave on HIGH for 15 mins, covered.

3. Blend together cornflour and water and stir into vegetable mixture.

4. Heat 4½—5½ mins on HIGH.

5. Stand for 10 mins and serve.

Lentil Soup

225 g (8 oz) lentils - soaked
2 medium onions - chopped
1 medium carrot - chopped
750 ml (1¼ pt) bacon stock (water and 2 bacon rashers)
Salt and pepper

1. Place lentils, onions, carrot and stock in bowl.

2. Microwave covered on HIGH for 18—21 mins.

3. Season and liquidise until smooth. Reheat for 2—3 mins before serving.

Cream of Leek and Potato Soup

350 g (12 oz) potatoes peeled and diced
450 g (1 lb) leeks chopped finely
50 g (2 oz) onion finely chopped
25 g (1 oz) margarine
600 ml (1 pt) chicken stock
150 ml (¼ pt) single cream
Seasoning
25 ml (1 fl oz) boiling water

1. Place the diced potato in the water and cook in a large bowl on HIGH for 6—7 mins - covered.

2. Drain the potatoes and mash.

Mushroom Soup

175 g (6 oz) mushrooms-thinly sliced
750 ml (1¼ pt) chicken stock
1 medium onion-chopped
150 ml (¼ pt) single cream
25 g (1 oz) margarine
Salt and pepper
2 x 15 ml tbsp cornflour
4 x 15 ml tbsp water

1. Place mushrooms, onions and marg. in bowl. Cook 2 mins. on HIGH.

2. Add stock and cook on HIGH for 6 mins.

3. Thicken with cornflour.

4. Cook 1 min on HIGH. Then liquidise.

5. Stir in ¼ pt single cream.

6. Reheat on HIGH for 2—3 mins.

Cauliflower Soup

600 g (1¼ lbs) cauliflower cut into florets
25 ml (1 fl oz) water
25 g (1 oz) plain flour
600 ml (1 pt) milk
150 ml (¼ pt) chicken stock
Seasoning
Pinch nutmeg

1. Cook the cauliflower in the water covered with plastic wrap which has been pierced for 11—12 mins on HIGH.

2. Drain the cauliflower. Melt the margarine for 30 seconds on HIGH. Add the flour and the milk. Heat on HIGH for 5 mins until the sauce thickens slightly.

3. Puree the cauliflower through a sieve or use a blender or food processor.
Add to the sauce and place in a large bowl. Add the chicken stock. Season and add the pinch of nutmeg. Heat on MEDIUM HIGH for 5—6 mins.
Do not allow to boil.

3. Heat the margarine for 30 seconds on HIGH. Add the onions and leeks and cook for 2 mins on HIGH in a large bowl.

4. Add the chicken stock and cook for 10 mins on HIGH.

5. Add the potato and blend well into the stock and leeks.

6. Heat on HIGH for 3 mins.

7. Add the cream and heat for 2—3 mins on MEDIUM. Do not allow to boil. Stand for 5 mins.

Fish

Recipe Conversion to Microwave Cooking

If your recipe calls for poaching fish and then making a sauce with the broth, use only as much liquid as you will need for the sauce. When fish or seafood are cooked in a sauce, microwave the sauce first. Add fish or seafood toward the end of microwaving when they are combined with long-cooking ingredients.

Casseroles calling for cooked or canned ingredients will be done when heated through. When preparing uncooked fish or seafood, use a microwave recipe as a guide to time and check frequently to avoid overcooking. Loaves made with canned salmon or tuna usually need to change in ingredients.

Use HIGH (100%) unless the sauce is enriched with cream or eggs, which require a setting of MEDIUM-HIGH (70%) or lower. Stir seafood and casseroles when possible to speed cooking and help distribute heat.

Cod with Parsley Sauce

450 g (1 lb) Cod Steaks
50 g (2 oz) cheddar cheese, grated
300 ml (½ pt) milk
25 g (1 oz) flour
25 g (1 oz) margarine
15 g (½ oz) chopped parsley

1. Place fish into serving dish, cover and cook on HIGH for 3½—4 mins. Allow to stand.

2. Put the margarine in a 1-litre bowl or jug and heat on HIGH for 1 min or until melted. Stir in flour and milk. Heat on HIGH for 3½—4 mins until creamy.

3. Stir in chopped parsley and grated cheese.

4. Pour over cooked fish, garnish, and serve.

Tuna Loaf

  250 g (9 oz) canned tuna fish (drained)
  2 x 15 ml tbsp lemon juice
  150 ml (¼ pt) milk
  175 g (6 oz) fresh breadcrumbs
  2 eggs, size 3
  1 medium onion, chopped
  1 x 5 ml tsp salt
  ¼ x 5 ml tsp pepper
  1 x 15 ml tbsp dried parsley

1. Place tuna in a large bowl, sprinkle with lemon juice.
2. In a medium bowl mix milk, breadcrumbs, eggs, onion, salt, pepper and parsley. Pour over tuna fish and mix well.
3. Place mixture into a greased loaf dish. Heat, uncovered for 8—9 mins on HIGH.
                                              Serves 4—6.

Kedgeree

  1 pkt 225 g (8 oz) frozen smoked haddock
  100 g (4 oz) frozen peas or "leftovers"
  50 g (2 oz) butter or margarine
  1 large onion, chopped
  225 g (8 oz) long grain rice
  600 ml (1 pt) boiling water
  2 hard boiled eggs, chopped
  Salt and pepper to taste
  2 x 15 ml tbsp parsley

1. Place frozen fish on a plate, if "boil-in-bag" variety, pierce bag. Defrost on MEDIUM LOW for 4—4½ mins. Cook fish on HIGH for 3½ mins. Leave to cool, before removing skin.
2. Place frozen peas in a bowl. Defrost on MEDIUM LOW for 1½—2 mins.
3. Place butter in a large bowl, heat on HIGH for 2 mins. Add onion and cook for 3½ mins on HIGH. Stir in rice and boiling water. Cover and cook on HIGH for 11—13 mins. Stir halfway through cooking. Add peas and stir well. Leave covered for 6—8 mins.
4. Uncover dish, stir in eggs, seasoning and fish, and stir well. Cook for 4 mins on HIGH. Stir in half the parsley. Sprinkle remainder of parsley on top.   Serves 4.

Trout with Almonds and Orange

  2 medium trout
  25 g (1 oz) flaked almonds
  Juice of 1 orange
  Thin slices of orange for garnish
  Seasoning

1. Wash trout, place in dish and season.
2. Pour over the orange juice and sprinkle with flaked almonds.
3. Cook on HIGH for 3—4 mins, covered.
4. Garnish with orange slices and parsley.

Fishermans Supper

  3 tins of sardines in tomato sauce
  1 large onion - sliced into rings
  100 g (4 oz) peeled prawns
  100 g (4 oz) mushrooms - sliced thinly
  225 g (8 oz) wholemeal breadcrumbs (toasted)
  100 g (4 oz) cheddar cheese
  Seasoning

1. Layer the sardines, onion, mushrooms and prawns into a deep casserole dish, top with breadcrumbs and repeat layers again, finishing with breadcrumbs.
2. Microwave for 6—10 mins on HIGH.
3. Sprinkle the cheese over the top of finished dish and grill until brown 6—8 mins.

Plaice Stuffed Fillets

  225 g (8 oz) button mushroom - chopped
  100 g (4 oz) tomatoes
  100 g (4 oz) chopped onion
  2 x 15 ml tbsp chopped parsley
  Mixed herbs to taste
  8 plaice fillets (approx. 450 g (1 lb.))

1. Mix together the mushrooms, tomatoes, onion, parsley and mixed herbs in a bowl. And cook on HIGH for 4 mins. Place equal amounts of the mixture on each fillet and roll them up.
2. Arrange fillets in a non-metallic dish and remaining veg. around them.
3. Cover and microwave on HIGH for 6—8 mins.

Prawn Curry

  2 x 15 ml tbsp veg oil
  1 onion - roughly chopped
  1 carrot - cut into sticks
  1 x 15 ml tbsp curry powder
  25 g (1 oz) mushrooms - quartered
  ½ green pepper - cut in strips
  100 g (4 oz) pineapples - chopped
  150 ml (¼ pt) chicken stock
  2 x 15 ml tbsp cornflour (mixed with 2 x 15 ml tbsp stock)
  100 g (4 oz) peeled prawns
  Seasoning

1. In a casserole dish, heat the veg oil, 1 min on MEDIUM HIGH.
2. Add onion and curry powder and cook 2 mins on HIGH.
3. Add carrot, pepper, mushrooms, pineapple and stock and cook 4 mins on HIGH.
4. Stir in prawns and cornflour paste. Return to oven for 2—3 mins on HIGH.
5. Serve with rice and lemon wedges.

Fillet of Haddock with Broccoli

25 g (1 oz) butter or margarine
25 g (1 oz) flour
½ x 5 ml tsp salt
½ x 5 ml tsp tarragon
Little black pepper
300 ml (½ pt) milk
3 x 15 ml tbsp white wine
3 x 15 ml tbsp water
1 x 225 g (8 oz) pkt frozen broccoli
1 x 15 ml tbsp lemon juice
550 g (1¼ lb) fresh haddock fillets
Lemon juice
Salt & pepper to taste
1 x 15 ml tbsp Parmesan cheese

1. Place butter in a bowl and heat for 1 min on HIGH, or until melted. Add flour, salt, tarragon and black pepper, mix well. Heat for ½ min on HIGH. Slowly add milk, stirring constantly. Heat for 3½—4 mins on HIGH, stirring halfway through cooking. Add wine, stir and heat for further 2 mins on HIGH. Set aside.

2. Place water in a bowl. Chop frozen broccoli spears and add to water. Cover and cook for 3 mins on HIGH. Stir and cook for further 3 mins on HIGH. Drain.

3. Mix 150 ml (¼ pt) sauce with 1 x 15 ml tbsp lemon juice. Add broccoli and mix well.

4. Wash fish fillets, dry with kitchen paper. Divide into 4 portions. Overlap fillets on a large serving dish. Sprinkle with lemon juice, salt and pepper. Spoon remaining sauce over fish. Cook on HIGH for 5 mins.

5. Spoon broccoli mixture around edge of fish dish. Cook on HIGH for 4 mins. Sprinkle parmesan cheese over fish 1 min before end of cooking time.   Serves 4.

Sea Flan

175 g (6 oz) shortcrust pastry
2 cod steaks
100 g (4 oz) fresh or frozen prawns
300 ml (½ pt) cheese sauce (see page ??)
Garnish: 2 whole fresh prawns (optional)

1. Roll out pastry and line a 20 cm (8") flan dish. Bake blind for 3 mins on HIGH.

2. Cook cod on HIGH for 3 mins. Flake. Defrost prawns if frozen.

3. Make up cheese sauce, add cod and prawns to sauce and mix well. Pour into flan case. Bake for 10—14 mins on DUAL COOK (on 200°C microwave LOW).

Serves 4—6.

Microwaving is one of the easiest and most effective ways of preparing fish and seafood, which stay delicate and tender with quick, moist cooking. Overcooking dries out and toughens seafood, so you should check it after the minimum time. If thick pieces like fish steaks or lobster tails are done on the outside but still slightly translucent in the center, let them stand for a few minutes; internal heat will complete the cooking.

Sardine Quiche

175 g (6 oz) plain flour
75 g (3 oz) fat - (mixture of margarine and lard)
Pinch of salt
Water to bind
1 medium sized tin of sardines in oil (drained)
1 onion (finely chopped)
100g (4 oz) mushrooms sliced
Seasoning
150 ml (¼ pt) single cream
150 ml (¼ pt) milk
2 x size 3 eggs

1. Prepare shortcrust pastry by sieving the flour and salt together, rub in fat and bind with water.
2. Line a 22.5 cm (9") flan dish.
3. Layer sardines, onions, mushrooms and seasoning in flan dish; whisk together milk, cream and eggs and pour over sardine mixture.
4. Cook for 20—25 mins on DUAL COOK BAKE (on 200°C microwave MEDIUM LOW).

Herrings with Mustard Sauce

4 herrings - cleaned and gutted
25 g (1 oz) butter
25 g (1 oz) plain flour
300 ml (½ pt) milk
½ x 5 ml tsp mustard powder
Seasoning

1. Wash the herrings, place in a dish and cover. Cook on HIGH 6—8 mins.
2. Melt butter in a large jug for 30 seconds on HIGH. Add the flour and milk. Stir well. Add mustard.
3. Cook on HIGH for 3—3½ mins. Whisk well.
4. Drain fish, place on serving dish. Pour over the sauce and heat on MEDIUM HIGH for 2 mins. Serve.

Stuffed Mackerel

4 medium fresh mackerel cleaned and gutted
50 g (2 oz) onion finely chopped
50 g (2 oz) fresh white breadcrumbs
50 g (2 oz) chopped walnuts
1 large orange peeled and segmented
6 x 15 ml tbsp orange juice
1 x 5 ml tsp mixed herbs
Seasoning

1. Wash the fish.
2. Mix all the stuffing ingredients together. If necessary add more orange juice to bind together.
3. Divide the stuffing between four and stuff each fish with a quarter of the stuffing.

4. Place in the serving dish with 2 tbsp of the orange juice. Cover and cook on MEDIUM HIGH for 12—14 mins. Allow to stand for 5 minutes. Serves 10—12.

Creamed Haddock

350 g (12 oz) haddock
2 x 15 ml tbsp milk
15 g (½ oz) butter
2 eggs, hard boiled & chopped
3 tomatoes, skinned & chopped
300 ml (½ pt) parsley sauce — see page 101
Salt & pepper
50 g (2 oz) grated cheese
25 g (1 oz) fresh breadcrumbs
Garnish — olives and watercress

1. Place haddock, milk and butter in dish, cover and cook on HIGH for 3—4 mins. Remove fish and flake. Return to the dish with eggs, tomatoes, sauce and seasoning. Mix well. Sprinkle top with cheese and breadcrumbs.
2. Heat for 1—2 mins, or until cheese has melted. Garnish with olives and watercress.
Serves 4.

Poached Fish

450 g (1 lb) filleted fish
25 g (1 oz) butter
3 x 15 ml tbsp milk or white wine
Black pepper

1. Arrange fish in a large shallow dish. Dot the surface with butter, pour over wine and sprinkle with pepper.
2. Cover dish and cook on HIGH for 3—4 mins. Leave to stand.
Serves 4.

Tuna in Cream Sauce

50 g (2 oz) small mushrooms, sliced
1 green pepper, deseeded & diced
25 g (1 oz) butter
1 x 290 g (10.2 oz) can condensed mushroom soup
150 ml (¼ pt) single cream
Salt and pepper
1 x 175 g (7 oz) can tuna-flaked

1. Place mushrooms and pepper in a large dish with the butter, and heat, covered, on HIGH for 2 mins.
2. Blend in the soup, cream, seasoning and flaked tuna. Cook on MEDIUM HIGH for 4—5 mins until hot.
Serve with rice.
Serves 4.

Halibut Steaks with Tomatoes and Cream

25 g (1 oz) butter
1 large onion, thinly sliced and separated into rings.
1 x 400 g (14 oz) can tomatoes, chopped
1 x 5 ml tsp dried marjoram
½ x 5 ml tsp salt
¼ x 5 ml tsp black pepper
4 halibut steaks
225 g (8 oz) button mushrooms halved
150 ml (¼ pt) double cream

1. In a medium-sized bowl melt the butter on HIGH for 1 min. Add the onions and cook on HIGH stirring occasionally for 3½ mins, until soft. Stir in tomatoes and juice from can, marjoram salt and pepper.
2. Place fish steaks in a casserole dish and pour in the tomato mixture. Cook on HIGH for 10 mins.
3. Stir in the mushrooms and cream and cook on MEDIUM HIGH for 3—3½ mins until mushrooms are heated through. Do not allow to boil.

Trout and Almonds

2 medium size trout-cleaned
2 x 15 ml tbsp lemon juice
25 g (1 oz) butter or margarine
toasted almonds (See below)
Black pepper
Chopped parsley

1. Place trout on serving dish, cover with plastic wrap and heat on HIGH for 3—4 mins.
2. Put lemon juice, butter, almonds and pepper in a bowl. Heat on HIGH for 1 min. Mix well and pour over trout. Heat, uncovered for 1 min on HIGH. Sprinkle with chopped parsley.

Serves 2.

To Toast Almonds:

65 g (2½ oz) butter
65 g (2½ oz) blanched, sliced almonds

1. Melt butter on HIGH for 30 seconds.
2. Stir in almonds and heat, uncovered on HIGH for 2—4 mins until lightly browned. Stir occasionally.
3. Cool on kitchen paper.

Salmon and Hollandaise Sauce

4 salmon steaks, approx. 2½ cm (1'') thick
8 x 15 ml tbsp boiling water
1 x 15 ml tbsp lemon juice
½ x 5 ml tsp salt
Sauce: **150 g (5 oz) butter**
          Juice of ½ lemon
          2 egg yolks size 3
          Salt and pepper to taste
Garnish: **4 slices of lemon**
          Spring of parsley

1. Arrange steaks in a large shallow dish. Mix water, lemon juice and salt together. Pour over fish. Cover and cook on HIGH for 4—5 mins, or until liquid just comes to the boil. Leave to stand for 5 mins. Drain.
2. To make sauce, place butter in a dish and melt on HIGH for 1½—2 mins. Allow to cool slightly. Add strained lemon juice and egg yolks. Stir well. Cook uncovered on MEDIUM HIGH for 30—45 secs. The sauce is sufficiently cooked when it is thick enough to coat the back of the spoon. Stir sauce briefly, adjust seasoning.
3. Garnish fish with twists of lemon slices and parsley. Serve sauce separately.

Serves 4.

Meat

Goulash

450 g (1 lb) braising steak cut into ½'' cubes
25 g (1 oz) seasoned flour
225 g (8 oz) onions chopped
2 medium peppers deseeded and sliced
25 g (1 oz) oil
2 level 5 ml tsp paprika
3 x 15 ml tbsp tomato paste
Salt and pepper
50 g (2 oz) plain flour
2 large tomatoes, skinned and quartered
A bouquet garni
450 ml (¾ pt) beer

1. Coat the meat with seasoned flour.

2. MICROWAVE the onions and pepper in the oil for 2 mins on HIGH.

3. Add the meat and MICROWAVE on HIGH for 5 mins until brown in the casserole dish.

4. Add the remaining ingredients to the casserole.

5. Cover, cook for 35—40 mins on DUAL COOK (on 180°C microwave MEDIUM). Stir twice during cooking.

Lamb Hot Pot

4 lamb chops
1 medium onion - sliced
2 medium carrots - thinly sliced
2 medium potatoes - sliced
½ x 5 ml tsp marjoram
Salt and pepper
300 ml (½ pt) stock

1. Place lamb chops in base of a casserole dish. Sprinkle with salt and pepper and marjoram.

2. Arrange onions on top of meat and layer carrots on top of the onions.

3. Pour over the stock.

4. Arrange a layer of sliced potatoes overlapping slightly.

5. Cook for 40—45 mins on DUAL COOK BAKE (on 200°C microwave MEDIUM LOW).

Beef and Peppers in Red Wine

450 g (1 lb) braising steak
1 onion - chopped
1 stick celery - chopped
½ green pepper - deseeded and chopped
½ red pepper - deseeded and chopped
1 clove garlic - crushed
1 x 5 ml tsp mixed herbs
300 ml (½ pt) red wine
150 ml (¼ pt) beef stock
1 x 15 ml tbsp cornflour
Salt and pepper

1. Cut the braising steak into 2.5 cm (1'') cubes. Place in casserole.

2. Add the onion, celery and peppers and mix.

3. Blend the cornflour with the stock. Add the wine and pour over the beef and vegetables. Add the garlic and herbs. Season and cover.

4. Cook for 40—45 mins on DUAL COOK (on 180°C microwave MEDIUM), stirring twice during cooking. Serve with rice.

Steak and Kidney Pie

450 g (1 lb) stewing steak and kidney
1 large onion - chopped
450 ml (¾ pt) beef stock
2 x 15 ml tbsp cornflour
Salt and pepper
225 g (8 oz) puff pastry
1 egg to glaze

1. Cut up the steak and kidney into a casserole. Add the onion and stock. Season and cook for 30 mins on DUAL COOK (on 180°C microwave MEDIUM).

2. Blend in the cornflour to the stock and meat. Place in a pie dish.

3. Roll out the puff pastry to make the pie lid. Place over filling, damp the edges and trim. Use the trimmings to make pie decorations. Glaze with the egg.

4. Cook for 10—14 mins on DUAL COOK ROAST (on 230°C microwave MEDIUM).

Chilli Con Carne

450 g (1 lb) minced beef
1 large onion - chopped
1 x 397 g (14 oz) tin tomatoes
1 x 397 g (14 oz) tin of kidney beans
2 x 15 ml tbsp tomato puree
3 x 5 ml tsp chilli powder
1 x 15 ml tbsp worcester sauce
Salt and pepper

1. Place minced beef and onion in a casserole dish and cook together for 5 mins on HIGH.

2. Add all remaining ingredients, blend well, cover and cook on MEDIUM for 18—21 mins.

3. Stand covered for 5—7 mins.

Steak and Kidney Pudding

450 g (1 lb) stewing steak - cubed
100 g (4 oz) ox kidney - cubed
1 onion - chopped
½ x 5 ml (½ tsp) mixed herbs
12.5 g (½ oz) p. flour
400 ml (¾ pt) water
Pastry: 225 g (8 oz) self raising flour
  ½ x 5 ml tsp salt
  1 x 5 ml tsp baking powder
  100 g (4 oz) shredded suet
  Approx 125—150 ml (¼ pt) cold water

1. Place steak, kidney, chopped onion, herbs and water in a casserole dish.

2. Cook on MEDIUM for 60 mins, stirring half way through cooking. Add flour to thicken juices.

3. Meanwhile, make the pastry by sieving flour, salt and baking powder together in a bowl.

4. Stir in suet and mix to a soft dough with cold water. Knead lightly.

5. Roll out ⅔ rds of the pastry and line a 1 litre (1¾ pt) well greased pudding basin. Roll out remaining pastry into a circle.

6. Allow meat to stand for 10 mins before filling pudding basin cover with circle of pastry. Damp top of pastry. Make a small slit in the top to allow steam to escape. Cover with kitchen paper. Cook for 10—12 mins on HIGH.

7. Stand for 6 mins.

Sausage Plait

1 onion - chopped
50 g (2 oz) mushrooms - sliced
1 x 5 ml tsp mixed herbs
225 g (8 oz) puff pastry
225 g (8 oz) sausage meat
2 x 15 ml tbsp tomato puree
Salt and pepper
Egg for glazing

1. Place the chopped onion and sliced mushrooms into a heat proof dish and MICROWAVE on HIGH for 2 mins.

2. Add the sausage meat and MICROWAVE on HIGH for a further 5 mins, add tomato puree and seasoning to taste and allow to cool.

3. Roll out the pastry to a rectangle 30 cm x 15 cm (12" x 6") trim off the edges make cuts at an angle approximately 5 cm (2") apart.

4. Place the cool filling down the centre of the pastry; taking a strip of pastry from each alternate side. Plait across the filling. Place on a baking sheet and brush with beaten egg.

5. Cook for 10—15 mins on DUAL COOK ROAST (on 230°C microwave MEDIUM).

Beef with Mushrooms

600 g (1¼ lb) braising steak cut into 3.5 cm (1½") strips
225 g (8 oz) button mushrooms
1 small onion - chopped
1 clove garlic - crushed
3 x 15 ml tbsp tomato paste
1 x 5 ml tsp dried parsley
450 ml (¾ pt) beef stock
Salt and pepper

1. Cut the steak and place in a casserole dish. Place the button mushrooms in the dish. Add the onions and garlic.

2. Mix the stock, parsley and tomato paste together. Season. Pour over the meat and mushrooms, cover and cook for 40—45 mins on DUAL COOK (on 180°C microwave MEDIUM). Stir twice during cooking.

Pork and Apples in Cider

4 pork chops weight 550 g (1¼ lb)
1 large onion chopped
225 g (8 oz) baking apple
225 g (8 oz) sweetcorn
1 x 5 ml tsp tomato paste
½ x 5 ml tsp celery salt
2 x 5 ml tsp chives chopped (fresh or dry)
1 x 5 ml tsp chopped parsley
salt and pepper
300 ml (½ pt) medium sweet cider

1. Wash and place the pork chops in a large casserole dish. Add the chopped onion.

2. Peel core and slice the apple and place on top of the pork chops and onions. Add the sweetcorn.

3. In a basin, pour in the cider then add the tomato paste, celery salt, chives, parsley and salt and pepper. Mix altogether and then pour onto the prepared meat, onions apple and sweetcorn.

4. Cover and cook for 30—35 mins on DUAL COOK ROAST (on 230°C microwave MEDIUM).

Pork Chops with Orange Stuffing

4 medium sized pork chops
75 g (3 oz) fresh breadcrumbs
1 x 5 ml tsp parsley
Grated rind and juice of 1 orange
50 g (2 oz) sultanas
Salt and pepper to taste
1 egg (beaten)

1. Remove outside fat from the pork chops.

2. Slit each pork chop in half.

3. Mix together remaining ingredients.

4. Fill each pork chop with stuffing, place in flat dish.

5. Cook for 25—30 mins on DUAL COOK ROAST (on 230°C microwave MEDIUM).

Stuffed Peppers

4 green peppers
450 g (1 lb) minced beef
1 onion - finely chopped
2 x 15 ml tbsp tomato paste
1 cooking apple - finely chopped
½ x 5 ml tsp herbs
½ x 5 ml tsp black pepper
2 x 15 ml tbsp worcester sauce

1. Cut top off each green pepper, remove seeds and membranes.

2. Mix mince, onion, tomato paste, cooking apple, herbs, black pepper and worcester sauce together.

3. Spoon the mixture into the hollowed peppers, place on roasting rack. Cover loosely with plastic wrap.

4. Cook on HIGH for 13—16 mins.

Honey and Rosemary Lamb

1.6 kg (3½ lb) shoulder joint of lamb,
Salt and pepper
2 x 5 ml tsp of ground ginger
4 x 15 ml tbsp of clear honey
2 x 5 ml tsp of dried rosemary
450 mls (¾ pt) of medium cider

1. Place the joint in a roasting tin and rub with salt, pepper and the ginger.

2. Sprinkle with rosemary and run the honey over the joint of meat. Then pour the cider around the joint.

3. Cook for 47—52 mins on DUAL COOK (on 160°C microwave MEDIUM). Turn over halfway through cooking. Baste several times.

4. The residue meat juices can be used to make the gravy, if desired.

Greek Moussaka

375 g (¾ lb) minced lamb
1 large aubergine
1 x 15 ml tbsp olive oil
1 large onion
12 g (½ oz) margarine
1 x 200 g (7 oz) tin tomatoes
Black pepper
Celery salt (to taste)
3 x 15 ml tbsp single cream
40 g (1½ oz) grated cheddar cheese

1. Cook lamb for 2 mins on HIGH and drain away excess fat.
2. Slice aubergine thinly, place in a casserole dish with olive oil, cook on HIGH for 3 mins.
3. Finely dice onions, cook in margarine for 3 mins.
4. Place minced lamb and onions in layers over the aubergines. Season with black pepper and celery salt, add 1 small tin tomatoes, cook on MEDIUM HIGH for 27—32 mins.
5. Place single cream and cheese over the surface and cook for 10—15 mins on DUAL COOK (on 220°C microwave LOW).

Sausage Casserole

225 g (8 oz) sausages
1 cooking apple
5 rashers bacon
1 x 397 g (14 oz) tin tomatoes (drained)
1 x 200 g (7 oz) tin kidney beans
Black pepper
Mixed herbs (to taste)

1. Place sausages under grill for 7—8 mins and brown then place in the bottom of a casserole dish.
2. Slice cooking apple and place a layer over the sausages.
3. Place 2½ rashers of chopped bacon over the apple and season with black pepper and mixed herbs.
4. Layer with tomatoes and kidney beans and finally a layer of bacon and apple.
5. Season to taste and cook on MEDIUM HIGH for 18—20 mins.

Liver and Bacon

450 g (1 lb) lambs liver
lemon juice
Black pepper
4 rashers of bacon

Kidneys Turbigo

6 lambs kidneys
100 g (4 oz) small button mushrooms (halved)
25 g (1 oz) butter
1 onion - sliced
15 g (½ oz) flour
8 Chipolata sausages
4 x 15 ml tbsp red wine
4 x 15 ml tbsp stock
2 x 15 ml tbsp tomato paste
Salt and pepper

1. Skin, halve and core the kidneys, remove any fat or gristle.
2. Wash but do not peel the mushrooms, halve the mushrooms.
3. Place the kidneys and butter in a covered dish and cook for 4 mins on HIGH. Turn over halfway through cooking.
4. Cut sausages into 3 pieces and add with the kidneys and the rest of the ingredients to a large casserole dish.
5. Cover and cook for 6—7 mins on MEDIUM HIGH stirring halfway through cooking.

Serves 3—4

Liver Casserole

225 g (½ lb) lambs liver
1 small onion - chopped
½ green pepper - chopped
1 x 200 g (7 oz) tin tomatoes
100 g (4 oz) bacon rashers cut into 3
Salt and black pepper

1. Wash liver and chop bacon.
2. Place all ingredients into a casserole dish, cover and cook on HIGH for 5—6 mins.
3. Garnish with parsley and tomato.

1. Place liver in a dish, sprinkle with lemon juice and black pepper. Pierce membrane over liver to prevent exploding. Cook for 2—2½ mins on MEDIUM HIGH. Turn liver over and cook for a further 1½ mins.
2. Place bacon on a plate, cover with kitchen paper and cook for 2—3½ mins on HIGH.

Lasagne

450 g (1 lb) minced beef
1 x 400 g (14 oz) can chopped tomatoes
150 ml (¼ pt) stock
1 x 15 ml tbsp mixed herbs
½ green pepper - chopped
1 onion - chopped
175 g (6 oz) buitoni - no pre cook lasagne
50 g (2 oz) margarine
50 g (2 oz) flour
600 ml (1 pt) milk
75 g (3 oz) cheddar cheese - grated.

1. Place mince, tomatoes, stock, herbs and pepper into a large bowl and MICROWAVE on MEDIUM for 20 mins.

2. Melt butter in MICROWAVE on HIGH for 45 secs. Add flour and mix well. MICROWAVE on HIGH for 1 min.

3. Gradually beat in milk and MICROWAVE for 6 mins on HIGH beating once halfway through cooking. Add 50 g (2 oz) grated cheese.

4. In a casserole dish layer meat, lasagne and cheese sauce alternately, making two layers of each finishing off with grated cheese.

5. Sprinkle top with grated cheese.

6. Cook for 10—15 mins on DUAL COOK (on 200°C microwave LOW).

Lamb Stew

450 g (1 lb) stewing lamb
2 leeks-sliced
1 onion-chopped
2 carrots-chopped
150 ml (¼ pt) cider
150 ml (¼ pt) stock
1 x 5 ml tsp mixed herbs
15 g (½ oz) flour

1. Place meat, sliced leeks, chopped onions and chopped carrots in a large casserole dish.

2. Pour over the cider and stock and add the herbs. Stir well.

3. Cook for 40—45 mins on DUAL COOK (on 200°C microwave MEDIUM).

4. Combine flour with a little water and add to the casserole. Cook for a further.

Serves 4

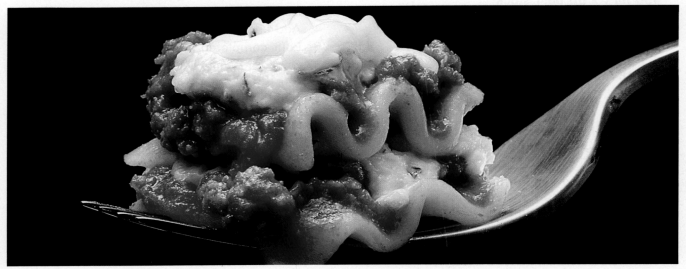

Sugar Baked Ham

1 piece of gammon ham approx. 1.3 kg (3 lb)
2 x 15 ml tbsp soft brown sugar
2 x 15 ml tbsp clear honey
225 g (8 oz) tin pineapple chunks
24 cloves
cherries to decorate
cocktail sticks

1. Place ham in a roasting tin. Score the rind and place the cloves into the rind.

2. Cook for 45—50 mins on DUAL COOK (on 180°C microwave MEDIUM).

3. 15 mins from the end of cooking take the ham out of the oven. Pour the honey over the scored rind, then sprinkle with brown sugar.

4. Place the pineapple chunks on cocktail sticks and spear into the rind. Then replace in the oven and continue cooking for the final 15 mins.

5. When cooked decorate the ham with glace cherries on cocktail sticks. Serve

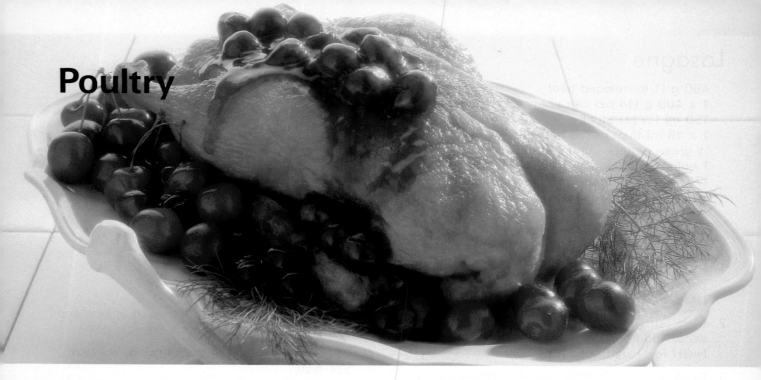

Poultry

Duck in Black Cherry Sauce

1 duck
1 large tin black cherries (drained)
150 ml (¼ pt) port wine
450 ml (¾ pt) beef stock
1 garlic clove crushed
25 g (1 oz) butter
salt and pepper
1 x 15 ml tbsp redcurrant jelly
1 x 15 ml tbsp plain flour

1. Blend the flour with the wine until a smooth consistency is reached.
2. Add the blended flour and wine together with the stock, garlic, butter and redcurrant jelly, stirring until all the ingredients are combined.
3. Add seasoning to taste.
4. Add cherries.
5. Pour completed sauce over prepared duck.
6. Cook for 8 mins per 1 lb/450 g on DUAL COOK (on 180°C microwave MEDIUM). Baste several time, turning over halfway through cooking.

Pheasant with White Wine and Orange

1 prepared and jointed pheasant
100 g (¼ lb) button mushrooms
50 g (2 oz) plain flour
300 ml (½ pt) orange juice
300 ml (½ pt) dry white wine
1 orange

1. Place pheasant joints into a casserole with the mushrooms.
2. Blend together flour and orange juice, pour into the casserole with white wine.
3. Cover and cook for 35—40 mins on DUAL COOK (on 180°C microwave MEDIUM).
4. Meanwhile peel zest from orange and cut into very thin strips.
5. Divide orange itself into segments.
6. Simmer strips of rind in water until soft.
7. Sprinkle over casserole before serving and garnish with orange segments.

Chicken in White Wine Sauce

1.3 kg (3 lb) chicken cut into 4 portions
1 med onion chopped
100 g (4 oz) button mushrooms
2 x 15 ml tbsp tomato paste
150 ml (¼ pt) white wine
150 ml (¼ pt) chicken stock
1 x 15 ml tbsp cornflour
½ x 5 ml tsp mixed herbs
1 x 5 ml tsp parsley chopped (or dried)
salt and pepper

1. Wash chicken portions and place in large casserole dish.
2. Cover with the onion and button mushrooms.
3. Mix the cornflour with 2 tbsp of stock. When smooth add the rest of the stock and wine. Then mix in the herbs, tomato paste and seasoning. Pour over the chicken.
4. Cook for 35—40 mins on DUAL COOK ROAST (on 230°C microwave MEDIUM).

Chicken and Mushroom Pie

225 g (8 oz) puff pastry
1 cooked chicken
225 g (8 oz) flat mushrooms
25 g (1 oz) butter
Salt and pepper
Pinch of ground mace
Pinch of cayenne pepper
3 drops of anchovy essence

White Sauce

1 x 15 ml tbsp dried parsley
25 g (1 oz) butter
25 g (1 oz) plain flour
300 ml (½ pt) stock
5 x 15 ml tbsp cream

1 egg beaten
Salt and pepper

1. Make the white sauce by melting the butter MICROWAVE on HIGH for 30 secs. Then add the flour and blend well. Add the stock and seasoning. Mix well and MICROWAVE on HIGH for 3½ mins.

2. Saute the mushrooms in the butter MICRO-WAVE for 2 mins on HIGH. Then season with salt and pepper and add the spices and anchovy essence.

3. Remove the meat from the chicken carcass in medium size pieces.

4. Add the parsley and cream to the white sauce. Arrange the chicken in layers in the pie dish with the mushrooms moistening well with the sauce.

5. Leave the chicken mixture until cold. Then cover with the rolled puff pastry. Glaze with egg.

6. Cook for 10—15 mins on DUAL COOK ROAST (on 230°C microwave MEDIUM).

Duck with Orange and Walnuts

4 duck portions
3 medium oranges
150 ml (¼ pt) white stock
1 x 5 ml tsp cornflour
50 g (2 oz) walnuts
Salt and black pepper

1. Thinly peel the rind from one orange and chop into 2.5 cm (1″) strips. Then squeeze the juice from 2 oranges. Slice the remaining orange thinly.
2. Place the duck portions in a casserole dish.
3. Mix the cornflour, stock and orange juice together and pour over the duck. Season. Cover.
4. Cook for 20 mins on DUAL COOK (on 180°C microwave MEDIUM).
5. Remove from the oven, take the covering off and baste the duck with the sauce. Lay the orange slices onto the duck and sprinkle the walnuts over. Cover.
6. Return to the oven and cook for a further 10—15 mins until the duck is cooked.
   Serve.

Turkey Sweet & Sour

225 g (8 oz) can pineapple chunks-drained
265 g (9½ oz) can bean sprouts-drained
1 large carrot, peeled & cut into thin strips
1 x 15 ml tbsp water
1 x 15 ml level tbsp cornflour
150 ml (¼ pt) malt vinegar
3 x 15 ml tbsp demerara sugar
Salt and pepper
2 x 15 ml tbsp tomato ketchup
450 g (1 lb) cooked turkey meat, cut into pieces

1. Drain pineapple chunks and bean sprouts, then make up pineapple juice to 150 ml (¼ pt) with the bean sprout juice.
2. Cook carrot strips in a covered dish with 1 x 15 ml tbsp water for 3 mins on HIGH, or until they are just cooked, then drain and leave to one side.
3. Mix cornflour to a smooth paste with a little pineapple juice. Add the rest of the juice, vinegar, sugar, salt and pepper, tomato ketchup and pineapple chunks. Heat on HIGH for 4½ mins or until mixture is just boiling.
4. Add carrots, bean sprouts and turkey meat and cook, covered for 5—7 mins on HIGH, to heat the meat thoroughly.
   Serve with plain boiled rice.

Serves 4.

Honeyed Chicken

4 chicken breasts
2 x 15 ml tbsp liquid honey
1 x 5 ml tsp mustard
½ x 5 ml tsp tarragon
1 x 15 ml tbsp tomato paste
150 ml (¼ pt) chicken stock
Salt and black pepper

1. Place the chicken breasts in a dish.
2. Mix all the other ingredients together and pour over the chicken.
3. Cook for 20—25 mins on DUAL COOK ROAST (on 230°C microwave MEDIUM). Coat the chicken with the sauce several times during cooking.

Marinated Chicken

600 g (1¼ lb) chicken pieces
2 x 15 ml tbsp olive oil
6 x 15 ml tbsp white wine
1 x 15 ml tbsp lemon juice
300 ml (½ pt) beer
½ x 5 ml tsp celery salt
½ x 5 ml tsp black pepper
¼ x 5 ml tsp mace
½ x 5 ml tsp ground garlic
¼ x 5 ml tsp salt
9 cloves

1. Mix all the marinade together and stand the chicken pieces in the marinade in a deep dish. Cover and refrigerate over night.
2. Drain the chicken from the marinade and place in a casserole dish. Add 6 tbsp of the marinade to the dish, cover and cook for 20—25 mins on DUAL COOK ROAST (on 230°C microwave MEDIUM).

Roast Duckling with Sage and Onion Stuffing

2 Kg (4½ lb) duckling
25 g (1 oz) butter
1 pkt 100 g (4 oz) sage & onion stuffing
300 ml (½ pt) boiling water
Salt for sprinkling

1. Wash and dry duckling. Place butter in dish and cook on HIGH until melted, approx. 30 secs. Add stuffing and water, mix well. Cook for 1 min. Allow to cool before stuffing the kneck of the duck.
2. Place duckling, breast side down on meat rack in a large dish. Cook for 20—25 mins on DUAL COOK (on 180°C microwave MEDIUM). Turn duckling over. Sprinkle the salt heavily over the breast. Cook for further 14—18 mins. Remove from oven, wrap in foil and stand for before serving.

Serves 4—6.

Coq Au Vin

50 g (2 oz) bacon- chopped
1 medium onion - peeled and sliced
1 clove garlic - minced
2 x 15 ml tbsp of plain flour
1 x 5 ml tsp salt
½ x 5 ml tsp black pepper
200 ml (7 fl oz) red wine
150 ml (¼ pt) water
4 chicken portions
225 g (8 oz) mushrooms sliced
1 bayleaf

1. Cook the bacon in a 3-litre casserole on HIGH for 2—3 mins until crisp.

2. Stir in the onion, garlic, flour, salt, pepper, wine and water. Add the chicken pieces, mushrooms and bay leaf. Cover.

3. Microwave on HIGH for 5 mins. Then cook on MEDIUM HIGH for 25—30 mins. Stir twice during cooking.

4. Stand 10 mins.

Chicken Curry

315 g (12 oz) cooked chicken
1 medium onion finely chopped
25 g (1 oz) margarine
1 medium cooking apple - peeled and chopped
25 g (1 oz) sultanas
1—3 x 5 ml tsp of curry powder or paste
  (according to taste)
300 ml (½ pt) chicken stock
¼ green pepper - deseeded and diced
¼ red pepper - deseeded and diced
1 clove garlic - crushed
½ x 5 ml tsp ground ginger
Seasoning

1. Melt the margarine in a large bowl for 30 secs on HIGH. Add the onion and cook for 2—3 mins on HIGH.

2. Add the apple, sultanas, garlic, ginger and curry powder. Stir and cook on HIGH for 3 mins.

3. Add the stock and chicken and cook on MEDIUM HIGH for 15 mins.

4. Stir, add the diced peppers and cook for 5 mins on HIGH.

5. Season to taste and serve with rice.

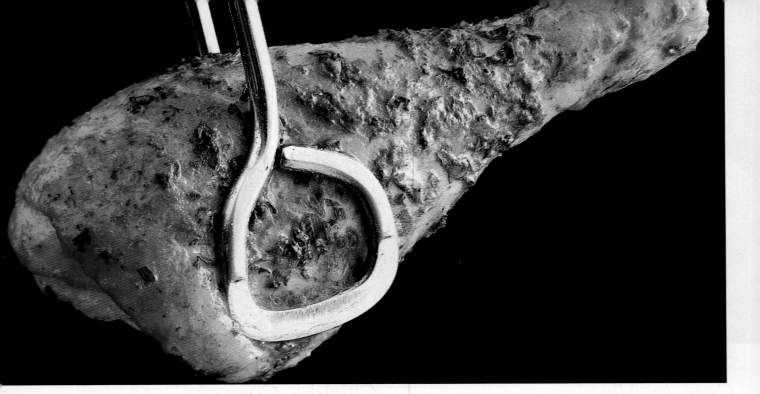

Herbed Drumsticks

50g (2 oz) butter or margarine
1 x 5 ml tsp dried tarragon
2 x 5 ml tsp chopped chives
1½ x 15 ml tbsp chopped parsley
Microwave seasoning
Salt and pepper
8 chicken drumsticks

1. In a shallow baking dish, melt the butter on HIGH for 1 min. Add herbs, salt and pepper. Stir thoroughly. Place drumsticks in baking dish and toss lightly to coat drumsticks well with the butter mixture.

2. Cook on Grill for 20—30 mins or until chicken is cooked. Turn drumsticks occasionally.

Serves 4.

Chicken and Mushroom Flan

1 x 8″ shortcrust pastry base
Filling: 175 g (6 oz) cooked chicken
50 g (2 oz) mushrooms
150 ml (¼ pt) milk
150 ml (¼ pt) cream
Salt and pepper
2 eggs

1. Line an 8″ dish with pastry.

2. Lay chopped chicken in the base of the cooked flan base, add ½ the mushrooms.

3. Blend together eggs, cream, milk and seasoning. Strain over the chicken and mushrooms.

4. Cook for 20—25 mins on DUAL COOK BAKE (on 200°C microwave MEDIUM LOW).

Chicken Cacciatore

225 g (8 oz) mushrooms sliced
1 medium onion - chopped
1 clove garlic - minced
4 x 15 ml tbsp tomato puree
150 ml (¼ pt) water
150 ml (¼ pt) red wine
1 x 5 ml tsp oregano
1 x 5 ml tsp parsley (dried)
1 x 5 ml tsp sugar
Seasoning
4 chicken portions

1. Cook mushrooms, garlic and onion in a large casserole on HIGH for 4—5 mins.

2. Stir in remaining ingredients except chicken. Then add the chicken, coating in the sauce.

3. Cook on MEDIUM HIGH for 25—30 mins. Stirring and coating the chicken twice during cooking time.

4. Stand 10 mins.

Rabbit Chasseur

1 rabbit, cut into serving portions
2 small onions, peeled and chopped
freshly ground black pepper
bay leaf
100 g (4 oz) button mushrooms
1 x 15 ml tbsp flour
450 ml (¾ pt) beef stock
200 g/1 small tin tomatoes
1 x 5 ml tsp mixed herbs
2 carrots peeled and sliced or 1 small tin carrots
salt
200 ml (⅓ pt) dry white wine
50 g (2 oz) butter
1 x 15 ml tbsp corn oil

1. Melt butter and oil for 30 secs on HIGH.

2. Add onions, carrots, mushrooms and cook on HIGH for 2 mins.

3. Sprinkle in flour and cook for further 1 min and stir.

4. Stir in the wine, stock and tomatoes return to oven and cook for 2 mins on HIGH.

5. Add the bay leaf, mixed herbs, salt and pepper to taste.

6. Pour the ingredients over the prepared rabbit, cover and cook for 35—40 mins on DUAL COOK ROAST (on 230°C microwave MEDIUM).

Turkey with Chestnut Stuffing

3.5 kg (8 lb) turkey
440 g (15½ oz) can whole chestnuts, drained and finely chopped
100 g (4 oz) fresh white breadcrumbs
225 g (8 oz) pork sausagemeat
50 g (2 oz) butter melted
1 piece celery chopped
1 medium onion, peeled and chopped
salt and pepper
1 egg beaten

1. Place the chestnuts in a bowl with the breadcrumbs and sausagemeat and stir well to mix.

2. Add the butter, celery and onion with the seasoning and mix.

3. Add the beaten egg and bind together.

4. Stuff the neck of the turkey with the prepared stuffing.

5. Then rub the turkey with butter on the breast.

6. Cook for 55—60 mins on DUAL COOK (on 200°C microwave MEDIUM HIGH).
    Turn over halfway through cooking.

Vegetables

Cauliflower Scramble

450 g (1 lb) cauliflower
300 ml (½ pt) cheese sauce
3 medium courgettes - sliced
50 g (2 oz) chopped onion
50 g (2 oz) margarine or butter
2 medium tomatoes, cut into 8 wedges
½ x 5 ml tsp salt
¼ x 5 ml tsp dried thyme

Makes 4 to 6 servings

1. Wash and divide cauliflower. Add 2 tbsp water and microwave at HIGH for 6 mins. Cover with cheese sauce. Set aside.

2. Combine courgette, onion and margarine in 2 litre casserole microwave at HIGH until vegetables are tender 3—4 mins. Stir in cauliflower, tomatoes, salt and thyme. Microwave covered at HIGH until heated through, 4—6 mins. Stir before serving.

Ratatouille

1 aubergine - sliced
1 medium chopped onion
1 large sliced courgette
1 x 397 g (14 oz) tin tomatoes
50 g (2 oz) whole green beans
1 clove garlic - crushed
½ red pepper deseeded and sliced
½ green pepper deseeded and sliced
Seasoning

1. Layer the vegetables in a large casserole dish. Pour over the tinned tomatoes. Add the garlic clove. Cover the dish with plastic wrap. Pierce and cook on MEDIUM HIGH for 14—16 mins, until vegetables are tender. Stand for 5 mins before serving.

German Potato Salad

6 slices bacon, chopped
50 g (2 oz) chopped spring onion or shallots
50 ml (2 fl oz) white wine vinegar
2 x 15 ml tbsp castor sugar
1 x 5 ml tsp salt
6 medium potatoes (approx. 1¼ Kg, (2½ lb)) peeled and cut into 6 mm (½'') slices
3 x 15 ml tbsp water

1. Place bacon and onion in a small bowl, cover and cook on HIGH until bacon is light brown, 5—7 mins. Stir in vinegar, sugar and salt. Set aside.

2. Place potato slices and water in a 2-litre (3½ pt) casserole. Cover. Cook on HIGH until potatoes are fork tender, 10—15 mins, stirring after half the cooking time. Drain. Pour bacon and vinegar mixture over potato slices. Toss to coat.

Green Beans Almondine

750 g (1¾ lb) fresh green beans
300 ml (10 fl oz) hot water
1 x 5 ml tsp salt
Flaked almonds
3 x 15 ml tbsp margarine or butter
¼ x 5 ml tsp ground nutmeg (optional)
¼ x 5 ml tsp pepper

1. Wash beans and break off ends. Break beans into 2.5 cm pieces. Place beans in a 2-litre casserole. Stir water and salt until salt is dissolved. Stir into beans. Cover.

2. Microwave on HIGH until beans are tender crisp, 9—13 mins, stirring once. Let stand 2—3 mins. Drain.

3. Mix in almonds, margarine, nutmeg and pepper until margarine is melted. Microwave on HIGH until heated through, 1 min.

Sauté Green Beans

750 g (1¾ lb) fresh green beans
50 g (2 oz) margarine or butter
½ x 5 ml tsp salt
¼ x 5 ml tsp dried savory leaves
⅛ x 5 ml tsp dried oregano leaves
⅛ x 5 ml tsp pepper

Makes 4 to 6 servings

1. Wash beans and break off ends. Break beans into 2.5 cm pieces. Place in 2-litre casserole. Place margarine in small bowl or 2-cup measure. Microwave on HIGH until melted, 1—1½ mins. Blend in remaining ingredients.

2. Pour seasoned margarine mixture over beans. Toss to coat. Cover. Microwave on HIGH until beans are tender crisp, 9—13 mins, stirring once. Cover; let stand 2—3 mins.

Sunshine Brussel Sprouts

450 g (1 lb) brussel sprouts
1 x 15 ml tbsp water
100 g (4 oz) onions
15 g (½ oz) margarine
100 ml (4 fl oz) milk and lemon
1 egg yolk
1 x 15 ml tbsp corn flour
1 x 15 ml tbsp lemon juice
Salt and Pepper

1. Place Brussel sprouts and water into 1½-litre casserole, cover. Microwave on HIGH until tender 5—6 mins. Stirring after half the cooking time drain and set aside.

2. Place onion and margarine into dish and cook on HIGH until onion is tender 3 mins. Blend in remaining ingredients. Reduse power to MEDIUM HIGH. Microwave until thickened, 1—2 min. Stir half way through cooking.

3. Pour over brussel sprouts micorwave on HIGH until heated through 1 min.

Courgettes à La Greque

2 x 15 ml tbsp oil
25 g (1 oz) butter
450 g (1 lb) courgettes, sliced
2 cloves garlic, crushed
4 tomatoes, skinned and sliced
100 g (4 oz) mushrooms, sliced
Salt and pepper

1. Heat oil and butter for 1 min. Add courgettes and garlic, mix well. Cover and cook for 2 mins.

2. Add tomatoes mushrooms and seasoning. Mix well. Cover and cook for further 5—7 mins, until all vegetables are tender.

Serves 4.

Farmhouse Casserole

450 g (1 lb) baby onions-peeled
25 g (1 oz) butter
salt and pepper
½ level 5 ml tsp dried mustard
2 large tins tomatoes drained and chopped
75 g (3 oz) breadcrumbs
75 g (3 oz) grated cheese
25 g (1 oz) melted butter

1. Saute the onions in butter for 8 mins on HIGH.

2. Season. Put the onion into a greased casserole.

3. Add the tomatoes. Mix together breadcrumbs, cheese and mustard.

4. Place over the mixture.

5. Pour over the melted butter.

6. Cook for 10—15 mins on DUAL COOK ROAST (on 230°C microwave MEDIUM).

Onions in White Wine

450 g (1 lb) small baby onions-peeled
25 g (1 oz) butter
1 level 5 ml tsp honey
Sweet white wine
Seasoning

1. Place prepared onions in a casserole.

2. Pour the wine over, and cover casserole.

3. Cook for 15—20 mins on DUAL COOK ROAST (on 230°C microwave MEDIUM).

Baked Carrots

675 g (1½ lb) carrots
3 x 15 ml tbsp water
3 x 15 ml tbsp oil
3 x 15 ml tbsp honey
1 x 5 ml tsp ground cloves
Worcestershire sauce, to taste

1. Chop carrots into small sticks.
2. Mix water, oil, honey and seasonings.
3. Put carrots into dish, pour over the prepared mixture.
4. Bake for 20—25 mins on DUAL COOK BAKE (on 200°C microwave MEDIUM LOW). Stir once during cooking.

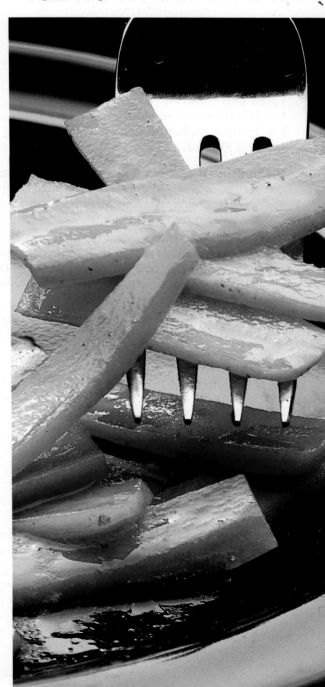

Celery with Bacon and Cider

1 head of celery
25 g (1 oz) butter
salt and black pepper
½ level 5 ml tsp cinnamon
240 ml (8 fl oz) cider
2 or 3 rashers of streaky bacon

1. Wash the celery and roughly chop.
2. Place the butter in an ovenproof dish.
3. Place celery in dish and add seasonings.
4. Pour the cider over.
5. Cut bacon into thin strips cook on HIGH for 2 mins. Lay the strips over the celery.
6. Put lid on dish and cook for 15—20 mins on DUAL COOK ROAST (on 230°C microwave MEDIUM).

Roast Potatoes

1 kg (2¼ lb) potatoes
3 x 15 ml tbsp oil
salt

1. Peel the potatoes and cut into 5cm (2″) pieces. Toss in the oil and place on the baking trivet. Sprinkle with salt and then place the trivet in the oven.
2. Roast the potatoes for 20—25 mins on DUAL COOK (on 250°C microwave MEDIUM HIGH).

French Baked Potatoes with Cheese

450 g (1 lb) new potatoes - sliced
150 ml (¼ pt) single cream
75 g (3 oz) grated cheese
25 g (1 oz) butter
Salt and freshly ground pepper (seasoning)

1. Place the sliced potatoes into a dish. Pour over the cream.
2. Sprinkle over the cheese. Dot with butter.
3. Cook for 17—22 mins on DUAL COOK BAKE (on 200°C microwave MEDIUM LOW).

Country Scalloped Potatoes

450 g (1 lb) potatoes
100 g (4 oz) mushrooms, sliced
12 g (½ oz) butter
100 g (4 oz) bacon
Cheese Sauce

40 g (1½ oz) butter
40 g (1½ oz) flour
1 x 5 ml tsp made mustard
  a grating of nutmeg
425 ml (¾ pt) milk
50 g (2 oz) grated cheese

1. Peel and slice potatoes into a 25cm (10″) shallow oven proof dish. Add 2 tbsp water, cover and microwave on HIGH for 5—6 mins. Drain.
2. Slice the mushrooms and saute in butter for 1½ mins on HIGH.
3. Cook the bacon on HIGH for 2 mins, then chop into small pieces.
4. Cover the cooked potatoes with mushrooms and bacon.
5. For the sauce - melt the butter on HIGH for 30—45 secs. Add the flour. Heat the milk for 3—4 mins on HIGH. Gradually blend in the milk. Return to the oven for 1½ mins on HIGH. Stir in half the cheese.
6. Pour sauce over potatoes, sprinkle with remaining cheese. Grill for 7—8 mins until sufficiently brown.

Cereals and Grain

Quick Cooked Rice

100 g (4 oz) bag quick cook rice
600 ml (1 pt) hot water
1 x 5 ml tsp salt

Serves 2.

1. Put the hot water and salt in a 1.95 litre (3½ pt) bowl and heat on HIGH for 4—5 mins or until boiling.

2. Place unopened bag of rice in the water and heat on HIGH for 4—5 mins until boiling. Heat a further 15 mins on MEDIUM until rice is cooked.

3. Drain and serve.

Rice Pilaf

2 x 15 ml tbsp chopped onion
2 x 15 ml tbsp chopped celery
2 x 15 ml tbsp chopped green pepper
2 x 15 ml tbsp margarine or butter
300 ml (½ pt) hot water
100 g (4 oz) sliced mushrooms
75 g (3 oz) uncooked long grain rice
1 chicken stock cube crumbled

1. Combine onion, celery, green pepper and margarine in 1-litre (1¾ pt) casserole. Cook on HIGH until vegetables are tender-crisp, 3—5 mins. Stir in remaining ingredients. Cover.

2. Cook on HIGH for 5 mins. Reduce power to MEDIUM. Cook until liquid is absorbed, 10—12 mins. Let stand, covered, 5 mins. Fluff with fork before serving.

Serves 2—3.

Fried Rice

2 x 15 ml tbsp chopped onion
1 x 15 ml tbsp margarine or butter
2 chicken stock cubes
600 ml (1 pt) hot water
450 g (1 lb) quickcook long grain rice
2 x 15 ml tbsp finely chopped shallots or
    spring onions
2 eggs, beaten - size 3
1 x 15 ml tbsp plus 2 x 5 ml tsp soy sauce

1. Combine onion and margarine in a 2-litre (3½ pt) casserole. Cook on HIGH until onion is tender, 3 mins. Set aside.

2. Stir stock cubes into hot water until dissolved. Add stock, rice and shallots to casserole, cover, cook on HIGH until liquid is absorbed, 7—9 mins.

3. Stir in eggs and soy sauce. Cook, uncovered, on HIGH until eggs are set, 2—4 mins, stir several times during cooking. Fluff with a fork before serving.

Serves 4—6.

Long Grain Rice

225 g (8 oz) uncooked long grain rice
600 ml (1 pt) hot water
1 x 5 ml tbsp margarine or butter (optional)
1 x 5 ml tsp salt

1. Combine all ingredients in a 2-litre (3½ pt) casserole.

2. Cover and cook on HIGH for 5 mins. Reduce power to MEDIUM. Cook until liquid is absorbed and rice is tender, 10—13 mins. Fluff with fork before serving.

Serves 4.

Porridge

3 cups hot water
½ x 5 ml tsp salt
1 cup quick porridge oats

1. Place water and salt in a deep 2-litre (3½ pt) bowl. Heat on HIGH until boiling, 4—4½ mins. Stir in porridge oats.

2. Cook on HIGH until desired thickness, 4—4½ mins. Stir before serving.

Serves 2—3.

Brown Rice

600 ml (1 pt) hot water
200 g (7 oz) long grain brown rice
1 x 15 ml tbsp margarine or butter
1 x 5 ml tsp salt

1. Combine all ingredients in a 3-litre (5 pt) casserole.

2. Cover and cook on HIGH for 5 mins. Reduce power to MEDIUM. Cook until liquid is absorbed about 30 mins.

3. Fluff with fork before serving.

Serves 4.

Spaghetti Carbonara

225 g (8 oz) tin cooked ham (chopped)
225 g (8 oz) spaghetti
600 ml (1 pt) boiling water
3 x 15 ml tbsp double cream
2 eggs (size 3)
Parmesan cheese

1. Soften spaghetti in boiling water, add chopped ham, cook uncovered for 10—15 mins on HIGH or until the spaghetti has absorbed all the water.

2. Leave to stand for 10 mins.

3. Beat rest of ingredients together, add to the spaghetti mixture.

4. Return to microwave, cook uncovered for 2 mins on HIGH.

5. Grate parmesan cheese over the top.

Macaroni, Spaghetti and Noodles

1 litre (1¾ pt) hot water
1 x 5 ml tsp salt
225 g (8 oz) Macaroni, spaghetti, noodles etc.
25 g (1 oz) butter or margarine

1. Mix water and salt in a deep 3-litre (5¼ pt) bowl. Bring water to boil, approx. 6—8 mins on HIGH.

2. Add pasta and stir. Cook on HIGH for 14—15 mins or until completely cooked.

3. Drain and toss pasta in 25 g (1 oz) butter or margarine if desired.

Cheese & Egg Dishes

Cheese and Mushroom Pie

**50 g (2 oz) bacon cut into small
  pieces**
175 g (6 oz) mushrooms, sliced
**3 x 15 ml tbsp (1½ oz) butter
  or margarine**
25 g (1 oz) cornflour
1 x 5 ml tsp curry powder
300 ml (½ pt) milk
100 g (4 oz) grated cheese
225 g (8 oz) short crust pastry
Salt and pepper
2 tomatoes

1. Place the bacon in a heat resistant container and cook on HIGH for 2 mins. Remove bacon from fat and leave on one side. Add the mushrooms with 1½ x 5 ml tsp (½ oz) butter and cook on HIGH for 1½ mins. Leave on one side.

2. Put 2 x 15 ml tbsp (1 oz) butter or margarine in a heat resistant bowl and heat on HIGH for 1 min or until melted. Stir in the cornflour and curry powder mixing well. Add milk and stir to a smooth consistency. Cook on HIGH for 3½ mins, stirring well after half the cooking time. When the sauce has come to the boil and thickened, remove from the oven. Add 75 g (3 oz) grated cheese and the cooked bacon and mushrooms. Season well. Leave on one side.

3. Line a 21 cm (8") pie plate with the short crust pastry, prick well. Pour the sauce mixture into the baked shell. Sprinkle the remaining 25 g (1 oz) grated cheese over the top and decorate with the sliced tomato round the edge. Cook for 15—20 mins on DUAL COOK BAKE (on 200°C microwave MEDIUM LOW) until the cheese is melted and brown on top.

Baked Eggs

2 eggs size 3
Butter or margarine

1. Lightly grease two small glass dishes with butter or margarine. Break one egg into each dish and puncture the yolk with a cocktail stick.

2. Heat, covered with cling film on MEDIUM for 1¼—2¼ mins or until the egg appears almost cooked. Allow to stand for 1 min to finish cooking. Baked eggs can be chopped and used as garnish or in salads that call for chopped hard boiled eggs.

Serves 2.

Stilton and Onion Quiche

225 (8 oz) shortcrust pastry
1 onion
100g (4 oz) smoked bacon
100g (4 oz) stilton cheese (crumbled)
3 size 3 eggs
150 ml (¼ pt) milk
150 ml (¼ pt) double cream
Salt and pepper

1. Line a 20 cm (8") flan dish with the pastry.

2. Chop the onion and the bacon, cook together on HIGH in the Microwave for 3 mins.

3. Place the onion and bacon mixture in the base of the prepared case, sprinkle over the crumbled cheese.

4. Beat the eggs, milk, cream and seasonings together, pour over the other ingredients.

5. Cook for 20—25 mins on DUAL COOK BAKE (on 200°C microwave MEDIUM LOW).

Macaroni Cheese

175 g (6 oz) macaroni
35 g (1½ oz) butter or margarine
35 g (1½ oz) flour
600 ml (1 pt) milk
Salt and pepper
½ x 5 ml tsp mustard
175 g (6 oz) grated cheese
1 litre (2 pt) hot water
1 x 5 ml tsp salt

1. Mix the water and salt in a 3 litre (5 pt) heat resistant, non metallic bowl. Heat on HIGH for 6—8 mins, until water boils.

2. Add the macaroni and stir.

3. Heat on HIGH for 10—15 mins or until completely cooked.

4. Drain in a colander.

5. Put the butter or margarine in 1.5-litre (2 pt) bowl heat on HIGH until melted. Stir in the flour and blend in the milk. Heat on HIGH until thick 5—6 mins, stir after half the cooking time. Whisk in salt, pepper, mustard and half the cheese. Mix well. Add the macaroni.

6. Pour into 1.7-litre (3 pt) heat resistant, non metallic dish, sprinkle the remaining cheese over the top.

7. Brown under grill for 7—8 mins.

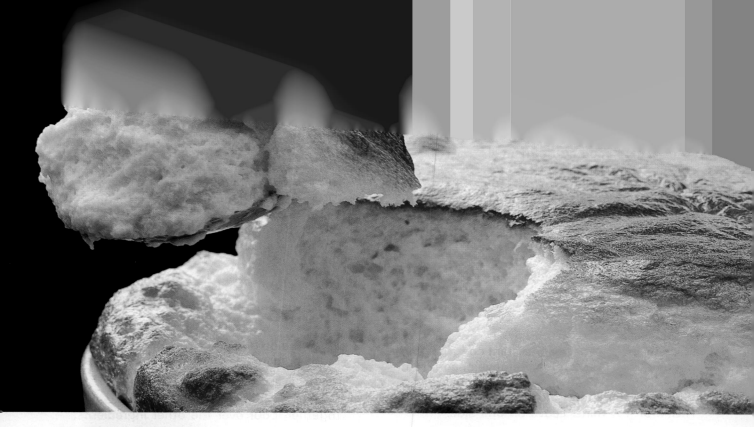

Cheese Souffle

60 g (2½ oz) margarine
60 g (2½ oz) plain flour
½ x 5 ml tsp salt
⅛ x 5 ml tsp cayenne pepper
375 ml (13 oz) milk
250 g (10 oz) grated cheese
6 eggs, separated

1. Place margarine in large bowl. Microwave at HIGH for 1 min until melted. Blend in flour, salt, and cayenne pepper. Gradually stir in milk. Microwave at MEDIUM HIGH until slightly thickened, about 6 mins, stirring every 2 mins. Add cheese, microwave at MEDIUM HIGH for 2 mins, stir to blend.

2. Beat egg yolks. Stir a small amount of hot sauce gradually into egg yolks, return to sauce, blending well. Cool slightly.

3. Beat egg whites until soft peaks form. With spatula fold egg whites into cheese sauce, half at a time just until blended. Pour into greased 2-litre souffle dish. Bake for 18—22 mins on DUAL COOK BAKE (on 200°C microwave MEDIUM LOW) until top is puffed and golden and centre is set. Serve immediately.

Serves 6

Egg Mornay

4 eggs
25 g (1 oz) flour
25 g (1 oz) butter
Salt and pepper
300 ml (½ pt) milk
50 g (2 oz) cheese (grated)

1. Bake eggs, by placing them in 4 individual ramekin dishes or cups, pierce each egg yolk lightly to prevent them bursting.

2. Cook on MEDIUM HIGH for 2—2½ mins.

3. Leave to stand for 1 min and turn out of dishes, meanwhile melt the butter on HIGH for 1 min or until melted, stir in flour and salt and pepper, cook for a further 30 seconds, stir in milk slowly, cook for 3—5 mins, stirring half way through or until thickened, add cheese and pour over eggs.

Yorkshire Puddings

300 ml (½ pt) milk
2 eggs
100 g (4 oz) flour
pinch salt
2 x 15 ml tbsp cooking oil

1. Brush 6 ramekin dishes with oil.

2. In a medium size bowl put the milk, eggs, salt and flour. Whisk until a smooth batter is formed. Alternatively, blend the ingredients in a food processor.

3. Pour equal amounts of the batter into each of the prepared dishes and place them into the oven and bake for 12—15 mins on DUAL COOK (on 250°C microwave LOW).

Scrambled Eggs

1 x 15 ml tbsp butter
4 eggs - size 3
2 x 15 ml tbsp milk
Seasoning

1. Place butter in dish, heat on HIGH for 30 secs or until butter melts. Add eggs and milk and beat with a fork.

2. Cook on HIGH for 2½—3½ mins, stirring at least once during cooking time.

3. Stop cooking while eggs look moist and soft, let stand for a couple of minutes, stir again.

Piperade

3 x 15 ml tbsp cooking oil
2 onions - finely sliced
2 cloves garlic (crushed)
2 red peppers, deseeded and sliced
4 tomatoes - skinned
4 eggs
Salt and black pepper

1. Heat the oil in a dish for 1½ mins, add the onions and garlic, cover and cook for 3 mins. Add the peppers and continue to cook for 3 mins.

2. Chop tomatoes and add to onions and peppers, season lightly and cover, cook for a further 3—4 mins until the vegetables are tender, stirring occasionally.

3. Whisk the eggs lightly and pour over the vegetables, stir lightly as for scrambled eggs, cover and cook for 1 min, stir then cook for a further 2—3 mins, when the eggs thicken the piperade is cooked.

Poached Eggs

425 ml (¾ pt) hot water
½ x 5 ml tsp white vinegar
½ x 5 ml tsp salt
2 eggs

1. Place the water, vinegar and salt into a deep 1-litre (2 pt) heat resistant non metallic bowl.

2. Heat uncovered on HIGH for 2—3 mins or until the water begins to boil.

3. Carefully break the eggs, one at a time into the liquid.

4. Heat, covered, on HIGH for 1 min (if using plastic wrap - puncture to prevent ballooning).

5. Leave to stand for 1 min or until eggs are done.

Cheese and Onion Pie

350 g (12 oz) shortcrust pastry
Filling
2 large onions, finely sliced
225 g (8 oz) Cheddar cheese, grated
25 g (1 oz) butter
1 x 15 ml tbsp Worcestershire sauce
½ x 5 ml tsp dried mustard

1. Line a pie or flan dish with two thirds of the pastry. Roll out the rest for the lid.

2. Mix onions and cheese, mustard and sauce.

3. Put filling into pastry case, dot with butter.

4. Place lid on top of pie press to seal. Glaze with beaten egg. Make a slit to let out steam.

5. Bake for 20—25 mins on DUAL COOK BAKE (on 200°C microwave MEDIUM LOW).

Puffy Omelette

1 x 15 ml tbsp margarine or butter
4 eggs
75 ml (⅛ pt) milk
¼ x 5 ml tsp baking powder
¼ x 5 ml tsp salt
Dash of pepper

Makes 2—4 servings

1. Place margarine in 23 cm pie plate. Microwave at HIGH until melted, 30—45 secs. Separate eggs, placing egg whites in large mixing bowl and egg yolks in medium bowl. Blend remaining ingredients into egg yolks. Beat whites with electric mixer until stiff but not dry.

2. Fold egg yolk mixture into beaten egg whites with spatula. Pour into pie plate. Microwave at MEDIUM until centre is set, 4—6 mins.

Cheese Omelette Variation: Sprinkle 225 g grated cheese over cooked omelette. Microwave at MEDIUM HIGH until cheese melts, 30 secs—1 min.

Mushroom Flan

225 g (8 oz) Shortcrust pastry
1 onion
100 g (4 oz) streaky bacon
3 size 3 eggs
Small can of mushroom soup
75 g (3 oz) grated red cheese
100g (4 oz) sliced mushrooms
Salt and pepper to taste

1. Line a 20 cm (8") flan with pastry, bake blind for.

2. Chop onion and bacon, microwave on HIGH for 3 mins, place in the base of the prepared flan dish.

3. Beat eggs together with mushroom soup, seasonings, half the cheese, add the mushrooms and pour into the flan dish.

4. Sprinkle the remainder of the cheese on top of the flan. Bake for 20—25 mins on DUAL COOK BAKE (on 200°C microwave MEDIUM LOW) until set and golden brown.

Quiche Lorraine

200 g (7½ oz) shortcrust pastry
1 onion, finely chopped
1 x 15 ml tbsp oil
100 g (4 oz) bacon, chopped
75 g (3 oz) cheese, grated
2 eggs
300 ml (½ pt) milk
1 x 5 ml tsp mixed herbs
salt and pepper

1. Line the flan ring with pastry.
2. Saute the onion in the oil for 3 mins on HIGH.
3. Cook the chopped bacon for 2 mins on HIGH.
4. Place the onion, bacon and grated cheese into flan case.
5. Beat together the eggs, milk, herbs and seasoning. Pour into flan case.
6. Place into oven. Bake for 20—25 mins on DUAL COOK BAKE (on 200°C microwave MEDIUM LOW).

Quick Bake Pizza

Base

200 g (8 oz) self-raising flour
½ x 5 ml tsp salt
6 x 15 ml tbsp oil
A little cold water

Filling

25 g (1 oz) butter or 1 x 15 ml tbsp of oil
2 small onions, finely chopped
1 small can of tomato puree
1 x 5 ml tsp oregano
75 g (3 oz) grated mozzarella cheese
175 g (6 oz) cooked ham-chopped

1. Cook onions with butter or oil on HIGH for 5 mins, add oregano.
2. Mix together flour, salt, and oil, and enough water to make a fairly stiff dough.
3. Roll out to approximately 22 cm (9'') in diameter.
   Cover base with tomato puree, onion and ham, and sprinkle with grated cheese.
4. Place in oven and cook for 12—17 mins on DUAL COOK BAKE (on 200°C microwave MEDIUM LOW).

Sauces

Basic White Sauce

25 g (1 oz) butter or margarine
25 g (1 oz) plain flour
300 ml (½ pt) milk
Salt and Pepper

1. Place butter or margarine in a bowl or jug and heat on HIGH for 30 secs until melted.

2. Stir in flour and blend in milk.

3. Heat on HIGH for 2½–3 mins until thickened. Whisk until smooth. Season.

Variations

Cheese Sauce: Stir in 75 g (3 oz) grated cheese and 1 x 5 ml tsp made mustard into finished sauce.

Mushroom Sauce: Stir in 50 g–100 g (2–4 oz) lightly cooked thinly sliced mushrooms into finished sauce.

Parsley Sauce: Stir in 1-2 x 15 ml tbsp chopped parsley into finished sauce.

Onion sauce: Stir in 1 large boiled and finely chopped onion into finished sauce.

Sweet White Sauce: Omit salt and pepper from basic sauce, stir in sugar to taste.

Bread Sauce

225 g (8 oz) finely chopped onion
350 g (12 oz) bread - cut into squares
50 g (2 oz) butter
300 ml (½ pt) milk
Seasoning

1. Melt butter for 30 seconds on HIGH. Add onion and cook 2–3 mins on HIGH.

2. Add bread and milk and cook 4–5 mins on MEDIUM HIGH.

3. Season and serve.

Brown Gravy

2 x 15 ml tbsp fat
300 ml (½ pt) cooking liquid or beef stock
2 x 15 ml tbsp plain flour
Salt and pepper

1. After roasting meat, pour cooking liquid into a jug. Skim off fat and discard apart from 2 tbsp.

2. Stir flour into melted fat and cook until browned, 3—4 mins on HIGH. Stir in the cooking liquid and cook on HIGH for 3 mins until thickened. Season.

Barbecue Sauce

1 medium onion, chopped
1 clove garlic, minced
1 x 15 ml tbsp vegetable oil
300 ml (½ pt) tomato sauce
50 g (2 oz) brown sugar
2 x 15 ml tbsp cider vinegar
¼ x 5 ml tsp dry mustard
¼ x 5 ml tsp salt
4 to 6 chops tabasco sauce

Makes 1⅔ cups

1. Combine onion, garlic and oil in 2-litre casserole. Microwave on HIGH until onion is tender, 2½—4½ mins, stirring once.

2. Stir in remaining ingredients. Microwave on HIGH until hot, 2—3 mins. Reduce power to MEDIUM HIGH. Microwave until flavors blend, 5 mins. Serve over meat.

Marmalade or Jam Sauce

1 x 15 ml tbsp marmalade or jam
1 x 5 ml tsp castor sugar
150 ml (¼ pt) water
½ x 5 ml tsp cornflour
A little lemon juice

1. Put marmalade or jam, sugar, and water in a glass bowl or jug and heat on HIGH for 1½ mins until boiling.

2. Mix cornflour with a little cold water and add to jam mixture. Heat on HIGH until boiling and clear. Add lemon juice.

Orange Glaze

125 g (5 oz) orange marmalade
125 g (5 oz) honey

Makes ½ cup

1. Combine marmalade and honey in small bowl.

2. Microwave on HIGH 1—2 mins. Use as a glaze on poultry.

Custard Sauce

1 x 15 ml tbsp custard powder
300 ml (½ pt) milk
1 x 15 ml tbsp sugar

1. Combine custard powder with milk in a large jug. Heat, uncovered on HIGH for 2½—3 mins.

2. When thickened, whisk in sugar until dissolved.

Chocolate Sauce

50 g (2 oz) unsweetened chocolate
200 ml (⅓ pt) water
1 x 5 ml level tsp cornflour
50 g (2 oz) sugar
Vanilla essence
25 g (1 oz) butter

1. Place broken chocolate and 100 ml water into a jug and melt on HIGH for 1½—2 mins.

2. Mix cornflour with a little of the remaining water, then boil the rest of the water and pour into the cornflour mixture. Cook on HIGH 1½—2 mins.

3. Add the melted chocolate and sugar and cook on HIGH for 1 min. Add vanilla essence and butter. Beat until smooth.

Preserves and Sweets

Cooking Hints to Microwave Cooking

Jams, marmalades and chutneys can be made quickly and easily in your microwave oven.
A large bowl or casserole two or three times as large as the volume of jam should be used, and small quantities made at a time. Preserves made in the microwave require less attention and will not burn the bottom of the container. For additional recipes follow the instructions for conventional jam or marmalade making, using the times and quantities of microwave recipes as a guide.
When making sweets or toffees use a dish two or three times as large as the volume of the mixture to allow boiling up. The mixture will not stick or burn.
NEVER USE A SUGAR THERMOMETER IN THE MICROWAVE OVEN.

When cool cover with waxed paper and cellophane or tight fitting lid.

Easy Pineapple Preserves

250 g (1 can) crushed pineapple, undrained
1 x 15 ml tbsp cornflour
2 x 15 ml tbsp honey
1 x 5 ml tsp grated orange peel

1. Mix all ingredients in deep 1-litre bowl.

2. Microwave on HIGH until thickened, 2—4 mins, stirring after half the cooking time. Pour into prepared jars, seal and refrigerate.

Apple Jam

2 medium apples, cored and peeled
350 g (12 oz) castor sugar
1 x 5 ml tsp lemon juice
2 fl oz water

1. Combine apples and sugar in medium bowl. Microwave on HIGH until apples are tender, 3—5 mins. Beat softened apple mixture with electric mixer until blended.

2. Microwave on HIGH until mixture is slightly thickened, 3—4 mins, stirring once during cooking time. Stir in lemon juice. Pour into prepared jars, seal and refrigerate.

Raspberry Jam Plus

600 g (1 lb 4 oz) frozen raspberries
600 g (1 lb 4 oz) castor sugar
1 x 15 ml tbsp lemon juice

1. Place frozen raspberries in 2-litre casserole. Microwave on HIGH until thawed, 2—4 mins. Stir in sugar and lemon juice. Microwave at HIGH until mixture boils, 8—10 mins stirring after half the cooking time.

2. Microwave on HIGH until mixture comes to a rolling boil, 3—4 mins. Microwave on HIGH to continue boiling, 1 min. Pour into prepared jars, seal and refrigerate.

102

Apricot Chutney

225 g (8 oz) dried apricots
175 g (6 oz) sultanas
75 g (3 oz) onion - chopped
1 x 5 ml tsp salt
½ x 5 ml tsp mixed spice
1 x 5 ml tsp ground ginger
¼ x 5 ml tsp cayenne pepper
100 g (4 oz) brown sugar
300 ml (½ pt) brown malt vinegar

1. Place dried apricots in a large bowl, cover with the water and cook uncovered for 6—7 mins on HIGH. Stand for 5 mins. Drain, but reserve syrup.

2. Chop apricots, add sultanas, onion, salt, spices and pepper and 2 x 15 ml tbsp of the apricot syrup. Cook, uncovered for 7—8 mins on HIGH.

3. Add sugar and vinegar and cook, uncovered for 15 mins on HIGH or until thickened. Stir twice during cooking.

4. Fill warm jars with chutney and cover. Makes approx. 1 Kg (2 lb).

Lemon Curd

100 g (4 oz) butter
3 eggs size 3
225 g (8 oz) castor sugar
Finely grated rind and juice of 3 lemons

1. Heat butter for 2—3 mins on HIGH until melted.

2. Beat remaining ingredients together and add to melted butter, stir well. Cook for 4½—5 mins on HIGH, stirring halfway through cooking time. When cooked sufficiently the curd should be thick enough to coat the back of a spoon.

3. Allow to cool slightly before transfering into warmed jars. Cover when cold. Makes approx. ½ kg (1 lb).

Plum Jam

450 g (1 lb) plums
Grated rind and juice of 1 small orange
2½ x 15 ml tbsp water
375 g (12 oz) granulated sugar

1. Halve and stone plums, place in a large dish with the water and microwave for 8—10 mins on HIGH until tender.

2. Add the sugar and stir.

3. Cook on HIGH for 2 mins. Stir.

4. Cook on HIGH for 8—10 mins stirring several times until setting point is reached.

5. Cool slightly and pot.

Three Fruit Marmalade

2 grapefruits
2 large lemons
2 oranges
850 ml (1½ pt) boiling water
1.8 kg (4 lb) sugar

1. Wash, dry fruit.

2. Squeeze out the juice and place in a large glass bowl.

3. Remove skins, pips, fruit skins and tie them in a piece of muslin.

4. Place peel in bowl with the juice and the bag or pith etc.

5. Shred the peel if desired.

6. Add ½ pint boiling water, leave for 1 hour. Remove pith.

7. Add the rest of the boiling water, cook for 15 mins on HIGH.

8. Add the sugar and stir until dissolved, cook for 20—25 mins on HIGH stirring every 5 mins until set.

9. Cool slightly before placing in pots.

Strawberry Jam

450 g (1 lb) strawberries
1 x 15 ml tbsp lemon juice
350 g (12 oz) sugar

1. Wash and hull strawberries. Put into a 2.8-litre (5 pt) mixing bowl with the lemon juice.

2. Cook on HIGH for 4½—5 mins, or until fruit is soft. Add sugar and stir well.

3. Cook on HIGH 11—12 mins, or until setting point is reached.

4. Cool slightly before putting in clean warm jars. Makes approx. ½ kg (1 lb). Cover.

Gooseberry Jam

450 (1 lb) gooseberries
200 ml (⅓ pt) water
450 g (1 lb) sugar

1. Prepare gooseberries and put into a 2.8-litre (5 pt) bowl with the water. Cook on HIGH for 12 mins or until fruit is soft and water is reduced to approx. ⅓ of quantity.

2. Add sugar and stir well. Cook uncovered, on HIGH for 9—10 mins or until setting point is reached.

3. Cool slightly before putting in clean warm jars. Makes approx. 675 g (1½ lb). Cover.

Fudge

350 g (12 oz) semi sweet or milk chocolate
   chips
200 g (1 can) condensed sweetened milk
25 g (1 oz) margarine or butter
100 g (4 oz) roughly chopped walnuts

1. Place all ingredients except nuts in large bowl.
2. Microwave at MEDIUM until chocolate melted, 3 to 5 mins, stirring once or twice cuting cooking. Stir in nuts. Pour into well-greased baking dish, 20 x 20 cm. Refrigerate until set.

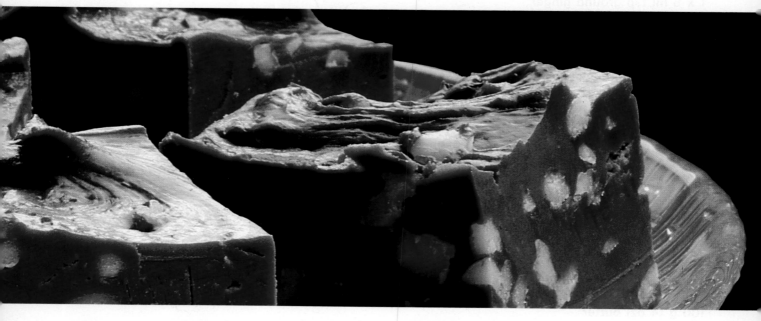

Rum Truffles

100 g (4 oz) plain chocolate
Rum essence
25 g (1 oz) butter
1 egg yolk
375 g (12 oz) icing sugar
2 x 15 ml tbsp milk
Chocolate vermicelli

1. Break chocolate and put into basin with butter, microwave on MEDIUM HIGH for 1½—2½ mins.
2. Stir in egg yolk, sugar, milk and rum essence. Mix well (The mix will firm up).
3. Roll into 24 balls and roll in the vermicelli, leave to harden off.

Toffee Apples

225 g (8 oz) demerara sugar
1 x 15 ml tbsp syrup
25 g (1 oz) butter
2 x 15 ml tbsp malt vinegar
5 x 15 ml tbsp water
4 eating apples

1. Place sugar, water, syrup, butter and vinegar in a bowl and heat on HIGH for 6—9 mins. Stir regularly until toffee reaches hard crack. Test toffee by dropping a little in cold water.
2. Dip the apples in the toffee mixture and leave on greaseproof paper to set.

Treacle Toffee

225 g (8 oz) demerara sugar
1 x 10 ml tsp treacle
25 g (1 oz) butter
2 x 15 ml tbsp vinegar
5 x 15 ml tbsp water

1. Dissolve the sugar, water, treacle, butter and vinegar together cook for 8—9 mins on HIGH until the toffee reaches the crack stage.
2. Pour into a greased tin and mark into squares. Allow to set 2—3 hours.

Peanut Brittle

75 g (3 oz) golden syrup
100 g (4 oz) castor sugar
4 x 15 ml tbsp water
1½ x 5 ml tsp baking powder
25 g (1 oz) margarine/butter
200 g (8 oz) shelled raw peanuts

1. Grease baking sheet heavily. Combine sugar, syrup and water in glass bowl. Microwave on HIGH for 3 mins stirring frequently.

2. Add baking powder and margarine and microwave on HIGH for 1 min.

3. Stir in peanuts and microwave at HIGH for 4—5 mins. Stirring after each 1—1½ mins until it reaches 'crack' stage.

4. Spread onto backing sheet. Cool and refrigerate. Break into pieces.

Desserts

Pear and Ginger Pudding

100 g (4 oz) flour
2 x 15 ml tbsp syrup
½ x 5 ml tsp bicarbonate of soda
¼ x 5 ml tsp ground nutmeg
120 ml (4 fl oz) milk
1 x 5 ml tsp ground ginger
50 g (2 oz) melted margarine (cooled)
2 x 5 ml tsp cinnamon
125 g (5 oz) golden brown sugar
6 canned pear halves
50 g (2 oz) golden brown sugar
25 g (1 oz) butter
25 g (1 oz) walnuts

1. Melt the butter for approx 1 min on MEDIUM HIGH, add the sugar and cook for further 1 min on MEDIUM HIGH.
2. Pour into greased 20 cm (8") tin square or round tin.
3. Arrange the pears and walnuts on top of the mixture.
4. Mix the flour, bicarbonate of soda and spices.
5. Mix together the egg, sugar, treacle, milk and melted margarine.
6. Stir into flour mixture.
7. Pour onto pears in tin and bake for 14—17 mins on DUAL COOK BAKE (on 200°C microwave MEDIUM LOW).

Treacle Tart

½ x 5 ml tsp salt
100 g (4 oz) plain flour
25 g (1 oz) lard
1 x 15 ml tbsp custard powder
25 g (1 oz) margarine
Milk to mix
225 g (8 oz) golden syrup
75 g (3 oz) fresh breadcrumbs

1. Make short crust pastry. Mix flour, custard powder and salt. Rub in fat and mix to a stiff dough with milk.
2. Line a greased 21.5 cm (8½ in) pie dish with pastry.
3. In a non-metallic bowl mix golden syrup and breadcrumbs together, heat on HIGH for 1½ mins. Add mixture to pastry case and bake for 15—18 mins on DUAL COOK BAKE (on 200°C microwave MEDIUM LOW).

Sultana Suet Pudding

100 g (4 oz) SR Flour
50 g (2 oz) shredded suet
50 g (2 oz) castor sugar
50 g (2 oz) sultanas
1 size 3 eggs
6 x 15 ml tbsp milk
Syrup

1. Place all dry ingredients into a bowl and mix well.
2. Add the egg and sufficient milk to make a very soft dough.
3. Place mixture into a pudding dish (1 pt) and cover loosely with plastic wrap.
4. Cook for 3 mins on HIGH.
5. Leave to stand then turn out and pour syrup over.

Apple Pie

250 g (10 oz) plain flour
125 g (5 oz) fat, half margarine, half lard
Cold water to mix
450 g (1 lb) cooking apples
Sugar to taste

1. Sieve the flour, cut the fat into cubes and rub into flour until the mixture resembles breadcrumbs. Add enough water to bind together and form a dough.
2. Line a pie plate (24 cm) with half the pastry. Roll out remaining pastry for pie crust.
3. Peel, core and slice the apples, place in a bowl and MICROWAVE on HIGH for 5 mins.
4. Place filling in pastry case, place the lid onto filling and trim edges. Crimp and seal. Brush with egg or milk.
5. Bake for 18—22 mins on DUAL COOK BAKE (on 200°C microwave MEDIUM LOW).

Traditional Rice Pudding

50 g (2 oz) short grain rice
25 g (1 oz) sugar
900 ml (1½ pt) milk
50 g (2 oz) raisins
1 x 5 ml tsp mixed spice
½ x 5 ml tsp ground cinnamon
1 x 5 ml tsp nutmeg
12 g (½ oz) butter

1. Wash rice and place in a 1½-litre (3 pt) dish; add the sugar and butter.
2. Pour in the milk, then add the raisins and spices. Stir.
3. Cook for 40—45 mins on DUAL COOK (on 160°C microwave MEDIUM LOW). Stir once during the cooking cycle.

Fruit Crumble

450 g (1 lb) fresh fruit
50 g (2 oz) brown sugar
½ x 5 ml tsp cinnamon
175 g (6 oz) wholemeal flour
A pinch salt
75 g (3 oz) butter or margarine
75 g (3 oz) brown sugar

1. Place fruit, sugar and cinnamon in a dish.

2. Sieve flour and salt into a large mixing bowl, rub in fat until mixture resembles fine breadcrumbs. Add sugar and mix well. Sprinkle over fruit.

3. Cook for 14—18 mins on DUAL COOK (on 200°C microwave MEDIUM).

Serves 4.

Chocolate Mousse

100 g (4 oz) chocolate
50 g (2 oz) castor sugar
300 ml (10fl oz) milk
4 egg yolks
1 x 5 ml tsp rum essence
300 ml (10fl oz) double cream

1. Melt chocolate, castor sugar and milk on HIGH for 2 mins.
2. Add egg yolks and Beat. Cook for a further 3½—4½ mins until mixture evenly coats the back of a spoon.
3. Leave to cool.
4. Whip double cream, fold into cooled chocolate mixture.
5. Place into individual dishes, leave to set.

Eves Pudding

2 baking apples
2 dessertspoons castor sugar
100 g (4 oz) margarine
100 g (4 oz) castor sugar
2 eggs
100 g (4 oz) S.R. Flour
1 x 15 ml tbsp cocoa
½ x 5 ml tsp baking powder
3 x 10 ml dessertspoon milk

1. Peel, core and slice apples, place in dish, cover with 2 dessertspoons of sugar, cook on HIGH for 5—6 mins.
2. Cream together margarine and castor sugar.
3. Add eggs slowly.
4. Sieve together flour, cocoa, baking powder, fold gently into mixture.
5. Fold milk into cake mix and spread over the stewed apples.
6. Cook for 10—14 mins on DUAL COOK BAKE (on 200°C microwave MEDIUM LOW).

Applestrudel

325 g (11 oz) plain flour
½ x 5 ml tsp salt
1 standard egg beaten
1 x 15 ml tbsp oil
150 ml (¼ pt) warm water

Filling

900 g (2 lb) cooking apples
100 g (4 oz) raisins
175 g (6 oz) castor sugar
½ x 5 ml tsp
50 g (2 oz) butter
icing sugar

1. Sift the flour and salt into a bowl and add the beaten egg, oil and water. Mix well.
2. Turn out onto a floured board and knead until smooth.
3. Place dough into a floured polythene bag and leave in a warm place for approx 1 hour.
4. Peel, core and thinly slice the apples, place in a bowl and mix raisins, sugar and cinnamon.
5. Place butter into a basin and cook on HIGH for 1 min or until melted.
6. Roll out the pastry to an oblong 20cm x 25cm (8" x 10") on a well floured board.
7. Gently stretch the pastry with the hands keep it as even as possible and taking care not to pull holes in it, until it reaches 38cm x 30cm (15" x 12"), cut off thick edges.
8. Brush the pastry with melted butter, spread over the prepared apples and raisins, roll up Swiss roll style, keeping the roll as tight as possible.
9. Place on prepared baking tray, brush with melted butter.
10. Bake for 15—20 mins on DUAL COOK BAKE (on 200°C microwave MEDIUM LOW).

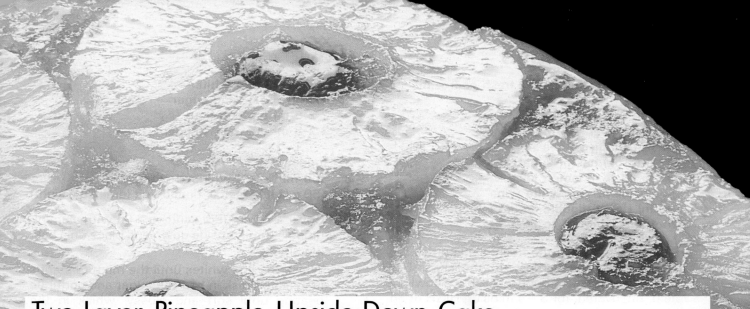

Two-Layer Pineapple Upside-Down Cake

1 can (485 g) crushed pineapple drained
1 x 15 ml tbsp cornflour
2 x 15 ml tbsp packed brown sugar
1 x 15 ml tbsp honey
½ x 5 ml tsp lemon juice
2 x 15 ml tbsp margarine or butter
50 g (2 oz) brown sugar
1 can (250 g) pineapple slices drainded (reserve juice)
7 glace cherries
225 g (8 oz) Victoria Sandwich cake mixture

1. Blend juice from crushed pineapple and cornflour in a small bowl. Stir in the crushed pineapple 2 tbsp of brown sugar, the honey and lemon juice. Cook on HIGH until thickened, 4—5 mins. Stirring after half the time, set aside. Place margarine in a round baking dish 23 x 4 cm (9'' x 1.5''). Cook on HIGH until melted 30—45 secs. Stir in 50 g (2 oz) of brown sugar spread evenly in dish. Arrange pineapple slices and cherries over brown sugar and set aside.

2. Line round baking dish 23cm x 4cm (9''x1.5'') with greaseproof paper. Add enough additional water to reserved juice from pineapple slices to equal amount of liquid required for the making of the sponge sandwich. Make cake mixture. Pour half of the mixture over paper lined baking dish and half over pineapple slices.

3. Cook first layer (paper lined baking dish) at MEDIUM HIGH 5 mins. Increase power to HIGH until a inserted scewer comes out clean 1—4 mins. Invert onto serving plate spread with crushed pineapple. Cook pineapple layer at MEDIUM HIGH 4 mins. until a inserted scewer comes out clean 5—8 mins. Cool 2 mins. Invert second layer on top of first.

Bramble Syllabub

450 g (1 lb) blackberries, fresh or frozen,
  thawed
1½ x 15 ml tbsp sugar
¾ x 5 ml level tsp ground mace
3 x size 3 egg whites
150 g (5 oz) castor sugar
2 x 15 ml tbsp lemon juice
150 ml (¼ pt) dry white wine
300 ml (½ pt) double cream whipped
Whole blackberries to decorate

1. Pick over and wash the fresh blackberries, dry well. Put the blackberries with the 1½ x 15 ml tbsp sugar and the ground mace into a bowl and heat, uncovered, for 3—4 mins on HIGH or until fruit is soft but still whole. Allow to cool.

2. Spoon fruit into the base of 8 stemmed glasses. Whisk egg whites stiffly, fold in castor sugar, lemon juice, wine and whipped cream using a metal spoon.

3. Spoon the mixture carefully over the fruit in the glasses. Chill for up to 1 hour and decorate with hole blackberries.

Note: This dessert is best made only 1—2 hours before serving, as the topping separates and becomes more liquid on standing.

Serves 8.

Jam Roly Poly

175 g (6 oz) self raising flour
Pinch of salt
75 g (3 oz) suet
6 x 15 ml tbsp hot water
6 x 15 ml tbsp jam
1 x 15 ml tbsp lemon juice

1. Mix together flour, salt and suet in a mixing bowl.

2. Add hot water and bind all ingredients together. Knead lightly into a ball.

3. Roll pastry out into an oblong approximately 35 cm x 18 cm (14" x 7").

4. Spread half of the jam over the pastry leaving a small border round the edge. Roll up lengthways and place on a large dinner plate. Form the roll into a ring, lightly pressing the two ends together.

5. Cook in microwave for 4½—5½ mins on HIGH.

6. Mix remaining jam and lemon juice together in a small bowl. Heat in microwave for 1 min on HIGH. Pour sauce over Roly Poly and serve.

Pavlova

3 x size 3 egg whites
175 g (6 oz) icing sugar
2 x 5 ml tsp cornflour
2 x 5 ml tsp malt vinegar

Topping
300 ml (½ pt) whipped cream
450 g (1 lb) Fresh or tinned fruit (drained weight)

1. Cover a 22 cm (9") sandwich tin with aluminium foil, turn it upside down and place on a baking sheet.

2. Whisk the egg whites until the mixture stands in peaks. Whisk in half the sugar and continue beating until soft and glossy, whisk in the vinegar.

3. Fold in remaining sugar and the cornflour.

4. Spoon 1/3rd of the meringue onto the upturned sandwich tin and smooth into a circle ½ cm (¼") thick. Place remaining meringue in a piping bag fitted with a large star nozzle and pipe a decorative border around the edge of the circle.

5. Cook for 1 hour on CONVECTION 130°C or until the pavlova is set.

6. When cold, pile the cream in the centre and decorate with the fruit.

7. The baked maringue base will keep in an airtight tin for 1 week.

Cremé Caramel

Caramel:	6 x 15 ml tbsp castor sugar
	3 x 15 ml tbsp hot water
Custard:	2 eggs size 3
	1½ x 15 ml tbsp castor sugar
	450 ml (¾ pt) milk

1. Mix sugar and water for caramel in a pudding basin. Cook for 5—6 mins or until caramel turns dark golden brown. Coat the sides and base of 4 ramekin dishes. Set aside to cool.

2. Lightly whisk together eggs and sugar, stir in milk. Pour mixture into ramekin dishes. Place in large dish. Pour almost boiling water into the dish, to reach the level of the custard. Cook for 7—8 mins on HIGH. Chill before turning out and serving.

Serves 4.

Baked Custard Tart

550 ml (1 pt) milk
4 eggs
50 g (2 oz) sugar
a little ground nutmeg
100 g (4 oz) shortcrust pastry

1. Line a fairly deep pie dish with the pastry (approx 23 cm or 7")

2. Whisk the eggs lightly with the sugar.

3. Warm the milk on microwave for 1 min on HIGH pour onto the egg mixture.

4. Strain the custard into the pastry case and sprinkle the surface with nutmeg.

5. Bake in the oven for 15—18 mins on DUAL COOK BAKE (on 200°C microwave MEDIUM LOW).

Bakewell Tart

100 g (4 oz) shortcrust pastry
35 g (1½ oz) margarine
50 g (2 oz) castor sugar
50 g (2 oz) cake crumbs
50 g (2 oz) ground almonds
½ x 5 ml tsp almond essence
2 x size 3 eggs (separated)
2 x 15 ml tbsp red jam
2 x 15 ml tbsp milk

1. Line a greased plate 19 cm x 2½ cm (7½" x 1") with the pastry. Prick well.

2. Cream together the margarine and sugar. Add the cake crumbs, ground almonds, almond essence, egg yolks and milk. Mix well. Beat the egg whites siffly and fold into mixture.

3. Spread the jam over the pastry base. Spoon the cake mixture over the jam in the pastry case.

4. Cook for 18—22 mins on DUAL COOK BAKE (on 200°C microwave MEDIUM LOW).

Peaches with Raspberry Sauce

4 peaches, peeled and cut into halves
1 x 385 g (13.5 oz) can raspberries - drained
2 x 5 ml tsp cornflour
½ x 5 ml tsp grated lemon rind
150 ml (¼ pt) whipping cream

1. Place peach halves in a baking dish, cover with plastic wrap. Cook on HIGH for 3—4 mins.

2. Drain raspberry juice into small bowl. Blend in the cornflour and lemon rind. Cook on MEDI-UM HIGH until thick, 2—3 mins, stirring during cooking.

3. Place 2 peach halves in each of 4 small bowls. Stir raspberries into the sauce and pour over the peaches.

4. Top with whipped cream if desired.

Serves 4.

Bananas in Rum

50 g (2 oz) butter
2 x 15 ml tbsp soft dark brown sugar
2 x 15 ml tbsp dark rum
4 bananas-peeled

1. Place butter in a shallow dish. Melt on HIGH for 1—1½ mins. Stir in sugar and rum. Cook on HIGH for 1 min.

2. Add peeled bananas. Baste with syrup. Cook for 4 mins, on HIGH.

Serves 4.

Stewed Fruit

450 g (1 lb) fruit, apples, plums, etc.
Sugar to taste

1. Wash and stone peel, or core fruit as required.

2. Place in casserole, add sugar to taste. Cover.

3. Cook for 4—5 mins on MEDIUM HIGH for plums, cherries, peaches, etc, or 6—8 mins on MEDIUM HIGH for apples and pears until tender.

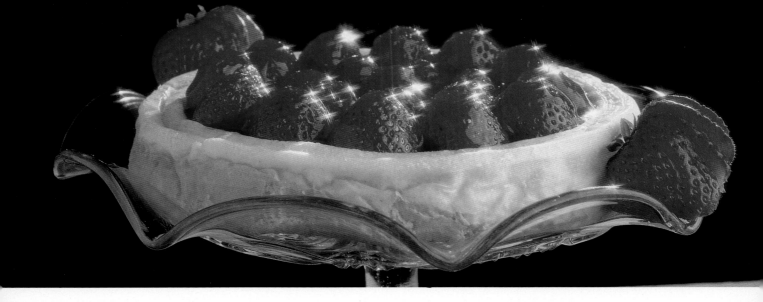

Strawberry Liqueur Flan

50 g (2 oz) plain flour
50 g (2 oz) castor sugar
2 eggs
few drops of vanilla essence

Filling

2 x 15 ml tbsp kirsh
200 g (7 oz) strawberries
2 x 15 ml tbsp redcurrant jelly

1. Place the eggs and sugar into a heat proof bowl, place the bowl over a second bowl containing boiling water. Whisk the eggs and sugar together until pale in colour and thick enough to leave a trail.

2. Remove the bowl from the lower container and sift the flour on top of the mixture. Carefully fold in with a metal spoon using a cutting motion.

3. Transfer the mixture into a prepared flan tin.

4. And bake for 7—10 mins on DUAL COOK BAKE (on 200°C microwave MEDIUM LOW).

5. Put 1 x 15 ml tbsp of the liqueur over the base of the flan case. Reserve about half of the best shaped strawberries for the decoration and thickly slice the remainder. Use these to fill the case.

6. Cut the reserved strawberries in half and use to decorate the top of the flan taking them to the edges.

7. Melt the redcurrant jelly and remaining liqueur on HIGH for 30 secs. Mix until smooth and carefully spoon or brush over the fruit. Allow to set for 1 hour before serving with whipped cream.

Christmas Pudding

75 g (3 oz) plain flour
50 g (2 oz) castor sugar
50 g (2 oz) brown sugar
375 g (12 oz) mixed dried fruit
2 dessert spoons of blacktreacle
2 size 3 eggs
2 x 15 ml tbsp brandy
2 x 15 ml tbsp brown ale
75 g (3 oz) shredded suet
75 g (3 oz) fresh breadcrumbs
50 g (2 oz) chopped almonds
Juice and grated rind of 1 orange
½ x 5 ml tsp mixed spices

1. Place dried fruit in a bowl, cover with boiling water and stand 1 hour. Strain the fruit.

2. Add the brandy and brown ale.

3. Add remaining ingredients to fruit mixture and stir well.

4. Grease 2 x 1 pint pudding basins and divide mixture evenly between them. Cover loosely with plastic barrier wrap.

5. Cook each pudding MEDIUM for 8—10 mins.

Note:
Storage; wrap pudding up in cling film or greaseproof paper then overwrap with aluminum foil, then store in refrigerator.
Reheating; cut pudding into individual slices, place on small plates and reheat 30—60 secs on HIGH depending on thickness and size.
Reheat whole pudding for 2—3 mins. (1—2 pt) Slice whole pudding for 1 min.

Strawberry Floating Island

2 eggs, size 3 separated
50 g (2 oz) castor sugar
1½ x 5 ml tsp cornflour
275 ml (½ pt) milk
½ x 5 ml tsp vanilla essence
3 x 15 ml tbsp castor sugar
½ x 5 ml tsp vanilla essence
450 g (1 lb) strawberries

1. Blend egg yolks, 50 g (2 oz) sugar and cornflour together. Gradually add milk. Cook on MEDIUM HIGH until mixture coats a metal spoon, 3—5 mins, stirring twice during cooking. Do not allow to boil. Add vanilla essence and chill.

2. Just before serving, beat egg whites until stiff but not dry. Beat in the 3 x 15 ml tbsp sugar, 1 x 15 ml tbsp at a time, until the mixture forms stiff peaks. Beat in ½ x 5 ml tsp vanilla essence.

3. Divide strawberries among 4 dessert dishes. Pour custard sauce over strawberries. Top each with a spoonful of the egg white.

4. Cook on MEDIUM HIGH for 1 min. Until egg whites set.

Serves 4.

Tipsy Tart

150 g (5 oz) chopped dates
150 ml (¼ pt) boiling water
½ x 5 ml tsp bicarbonate of soda
25 g (1 oz) butter
150 g (5 oz) sugar
1 x size 2 egg yolk
150 g (5 oz) plain flour
Pinch of salt
¼ x 5 ml tsp baking powder
50 g (2 oz) chopped walnuts

Sauce
150 g (5 oz) sugar
150 ml (¼ pt) cold water
Knob of butter
3 x 15 ml tbsp Brandy or Sherry

1. Place dates, water and bicarbonate of soda in a bowl and allow to soak for 10 — 15 mins.

2. Cream butter, sugar and egg yolk.

3. Sieve flour, salt and baking powder.

4. Add dry ingredients to creamed mixture, mix well. Add date mixture and walnuts, mix well.

5. Place mixture in a 21 cm (8'') flan dish. Bake for 15—20 mins on DUAL COOK BAKE (on 200°C microwave MEDIUM LOW).

6. Place sugar water and butter in a non metal dish, cook for 1½ mins on HIGH, stir, continue heating until sugar has dissolved, allow to boil for 7 mins, add brandy or sherry. Mark the tart into 8 wedges with a sharp knife. Pour sauce over. Serve cold. May be stored for 1 — 2 days before eating.

Continental Cheesecake

50 g (2 oz) butter or margarine
100 g (4 oz) digestive biscuits crushed
pinch of ground cinnamon

Filing

450 g (1 lb) cream cheese
100 g (4 oz) castor sugar
¼ x 5 ml tsp salt
100 ml (3½ fl oz) milk
2 x 15 ml tbsp lemon juice
3 large eggs

1. Microwave the butter, covered in a 23 cm (9") dish on HIGH for 45—60 secs, mix in the crumbs.
2. Press the crumb mixture firmly into the base of the dish microwave on HIGH for 1½ mins or until hot.
3. Microwave the cream cheese in a large bowl on MED for 1 min, stir in sugar, salt and milk. Whisk in lemon juice and eggs.
4. Microwave the filling on HIGH for 4 mins, stirring once, or until the mixture is like custard. Spread the filling over the crumb base.
5. Cook for 10—15 mins on DUAL COOK BAKE (on 200°C microwave MEDIUM LOW).
6. Chill for 2 hours before serving.

Bread and butter Pudding

6 thin slices of bread
50 g (2 oz) butter
50 g (2 oz) sultanas
50 g (2 oz) candid peel chopped
50 g (2 oz) castor sugar
2 size 2 eggs
300 ml (½ pt) milk

1. Preheat the oven to 200°C.
2. Remove crusts from the bread. Spread slices thickly with butter. Cut into fingers or small squares.
3. Put half the bread into a 1-litre (1¾ pt) buttered dish. Sprinkle with fruit, peel and half the sugar.
4. Top with remaining bread, buttered side uppermost. Sprinkle with the rest of the sugar.
5. Beat eggs and milk together. Strain into the dish over the bread. Leave to stand for 30 mins.
6. Bake for 14—18 mins on DUAL COOK BAKE (on 200°C microwave MEDIUM LOW) until the pudding is set and the top is crisp and golden.

Mille FeuiLLes (Cream Slice)

225 g (8 oz) frozen puff pastry (well chilled)
egg wash
100 g (4 oz) icing sugar for topping
filling optional i.e. jam and cream or fresh fruit

1. Roll out frozen pastry to approx. 18cm x 23cm (7" x 9") and divide into two portions.
2. Place onto a prepared greased baking sheet.
3. Bake for 8—11 mins on DUAL COOK BAKE (on 200°C microwave MEDIUM LOW).
4. Skim the prepared icing over the top of one portion and allow to set.
5. Cover the second portion with the filling and place the iced portion on top - serve.

Rich Gooseberry Pie

350 g (12 oz) shortcrust pastry
675 g (1½ lb) gooseberries
225 g (8 oz) brown sugar
25 g (1 oz) butter
beaten egg to glaze

1. Line a 20 cm (8") pie dish with half of the pastry.
2. Top and tail gooseberries and put into a bowl with 6 tbsp of water and sugar. Cook on HIGH for 6—7 mins. Stand for 4 mins.
3. Put through a sieve or puree in a blender. Then cut the butter into flakes and beat into fruit. Put into the pastry base and then roll out the remaining pastry and place on the pie base. Brush with beaten egg.
4. Cook for 15—20 mins on DUAL COOK BAKE (on 200°C microwave MEDIUM LOW).

Beryl's Pudding

675 g (1½ lb) mixed fresh fruit trimmed and washed
175 g (6 oz) fresh brown breadcrumbs
100 g (4 oz) demerara sugar
75 g (3 oz) suet
1 x 5 ml tsp all spice

1. Grease an ovenproof dish. Cut the fruit into blte size pieces.
2. Mix together the crumbs, sugar, suet and all spice.
3. Alternate layers of fruit and crumb mixture to the top of the dish.
4. Bake for 14—18 mins on DUAL COOK BAKE (on 200°C microwave MEDIUM LOW).

Sticky Orange Pudding

3 x 15 ml tbsp orange marmalade
2 medium oranges
100 g (4 oz) butter or margarine
100 g (4 oz) castor sugar
2 x size 2 eggs, beaten
75 g (3 oz) self raising flour
50 g (2 oz) fresh white bread crumbs
75 g (3 oz) glace cherries, roughly chopped
75 g (3 oz) sultanas

1. Spread base and sides of a 900 g (2 lb) loaf tin with marmalade.
2. Grate rind from one orange, and sequeeze juice from half an orange. Slice the remaining 1½ oranges, and arrange them along the sides and base of loaf tin.
3. Cream butter, sugar and orange rind until light and fluffy. Gradually beat in egg, beating well after each addition.
4. Mix flour and bread crumbs together, fold into creamed mixture. Stir in cherries, sultanas and orange juice.
5. Place mixture carefully in orange lined tin. Bake for 15—19 mins on DUAL COOK BAKE (on 200°C microwave MEDIUM LOW) or until a skewer inserted into the centre of the pudding comes out cleanly. Leave for 5 mins before turning out.

Serves 6 persons.

Chocolate Eclairs

Choux pastry
150 ml (¼ pt) water
50 g (2 oz) margarine
70 g (2½ oz) plain flour
Pinch salt
2 eggs size 3.

Filling
Double or whipping cream
Few drops of vanilla essence
2 x 15 ml tsp castor sugar

Topping
100 g (4 oz) plain chocolate
225 g (8 oz) icing sugar
2 x 15 ml tbsp water

1. Heat the water and margarine in a heat resistant bowl on HIGH for 1½—2 mins, until the fat melts and the water boils.

2. Add the flour and salt quickly and beat well. Heat uncovered on HIGH for 1 min, add the slightly beaten eggs and beat well.

3. Grease baking sheet, pipe the choux mixture in 10 cm (4″) lengths onto the baking sheet, using a forcing bag fitted with a plain 1.5 cm (½″) tube.

4. Bake for 17—22 mins on CONVECTION 200°C.

5. When cool split the eclairs in two and add the whipped cream flavoured with the sugar and vanilla essence.

6. To make the topping, break up the chocolate in to a bowl, microwave on HIGH for 2 mins. Sieve the icing sugar into a bowl, add the water until well mixed.

7. Add the softened chocolate and heat until smooth and shiny. Cover the top of each eclair with the icing. Allow to set on a wire tray.

Cakes and Biscuits

Cake Techniques

Layer Cakes. Use a mix or your own conventional recipe. If not done, let stand in oven a few minutes to complete cooking.

For perfect results the use of the metal racks is advisable, this allows the hot air to circulate around the food.

Victoria Sandwich Cake

175 g (6 oz) butter or margarine
175 g (6 oz) castor sugar
3 size 3 eggs
175 g (6 oz) self raising flour
2 tbsp (40 ml) jam
castor sugar to dredge

1. Grease and line two 18 cm (7") sandwich tins.
2. Cream the fat and the sugar until pale and fluffy.
3. Add the eggs one at a time, beating well after each addition, fold in the flour with a metal spoon.
4. Halve the mixture and divide between the two prepared tins and smooth the tops.
5. Bake the cakes for 18—22 mins on CONVECTION 180°C at until golden brown and firm to the touch.
6. Turn out and cool on a wire rack.
7. When the cakes are cool sandwich them together with jam and sprinkle the top with castor sugar.

Variation to the Basic Cake Mixture

Chocolate

Replace 3 level 15 ml tbsp of flour with 3 x 15 ml tbsp of cocoa. For a moisture cake blend the cocoa with water to give a thick paste, and beat into the creamed ingredients.

Coffee

Add 2 x 5 ml tsp instant coffee disolved in a little warm water add to the creamed mixture.

Rich Cherry Cake

225g (8 oz) plain flour
½ x 5 ml tsp salt
1 x 5 ml tsp baking powder
75g (3 oz) glace cherries
175g (6 oz) butter or margarine
175g (6 oz) castor sugar
2 x size 2 eggs beaten
Milk

1. Grease and line a 17.5 cm (7") cake tin.

2. Sieve flour, salt and baking powder.

3. Cut cherries into 4, and add to the flour.

4. Cream butter and sugar until light and fluffy. Gradually add eggs, beating well.

5. Fold in dry ingredients. Adding a little milk if necessary to form a soft consistency.

6. Bake for 15—19 mins on DUAL COOK BAKE (on 200°C microwave MEDIUM LOW) until a skewer inserted into the centre of the cake comes out cleanly.

Date and Walnut Loaf

150 g (2 oz) margarine
225 g (8 oz) plain flour
225 g (8 oz) dates, chopped
200 ml (⅓ pt) water
1 x 5 ml tsp bicarbonate of soda
175 g (6 oz) sugar
1 x 5 ml tsp baking powder
50 g (2 oz) walnuts, chopped
1 egg

1. Rub the fat into the flour. Soften the dates by pouring ⅓ pt of water with tsp bicarbonate over the top of the chopped dates.

2. Add sugar, baking powder, walnuts to the flour.

3. Pour in the softened date mixture, and add the egg.

4. Put into a greased 1 kg (2 lb) loaf tin.

5. Bake for 50—60 mins on CONVECTION 180°C.

6. Leave in the tin for 10 mins before turning out.

7. Can be served on its own or sliced and buttered.

Orange and Lemon Swirl

175 g (6 oz) margarine
175 g (6 oz) castor sugar
3 eggs size 3
175 g (6 oz) self raising flour
½ x 5 ml tsp baking powder
1 orange grated rind and juice extracted
1 lemon grated rind and juice extracted
Orange and yellow cochineal

1. Cream margarine and sugar together, add eggs gradually.

2. Sieve flour and baking powder together, fold into mixture.

3. Divide mixture equally into two, add orange rind and 1 tbsp orange with a few drops of cochineal if desired to one half, and lemon rind etc. to the other half.

4. Fill two piping bags with each mixture.

5. Pipe a ring of orange mixture followed by lemon etc. into an 20 cm (8") round cake tin. (Greased and lined).

6. Bake for 14—18 mins on DUAL COOK BAKE (on 200°C microwave MEDIUM LOW).

Topping: 2 tbsp lemon juice
         2 tbsp orange juice   mix together
         4 tbsp granulated sugar

7. Pour topping syrup over cooked cake.

Lattice Cake

100 g (4 oz) Butter
100 g (4 oz) castor sugar
100 g (4 oz) plain flour
50 g (2 oz) Ground almond
225 g (8 oz) mixed fruit
2 size 3 eggs
1 size 3 egg yolk

For the Lattice

100 g (4 oz) marzipan
50 g (2 oz) glace cherries halved
25 g (1 oz) walnut halves

1. Prepare a 19 cm (7½") loose bottom cake tin.
2. Cream butter and sugar together until fluffy. Gradually beat in the eggs, one at a time. Then beat in the extra egg yolk. Fold in the flour and ground almond and lastly the fruit. Turn the mixture into the prepared tin and level the surface.
3. Roll out the mazipan thinly, cut into strips and use to lattice the top of the cake. Fill each square with a halved cherry and walnut. Bake.
4. Bake for 14—18 mins on DUAL COOK BAKE (on 200°C microwave MEDIUM LOW).

Simnel Cake

50 g (2 oz) glace cherries, quartered
450 g (1 lb) almond paste
300 g (10 oz) currants
100 g (4 oz) sultanas
75 g (3 oz) mixed candied peel chopped
225 g (8 oz) plain flour
pinch of salt
½ x 5 ml tsp baking powder
3 x 5 ml tsp mixed spice
175 g (6 oz) butter
175 g (6 oz) soft brown sugar
3 size 3 eggs beaten
milk to mix
apricot jam

1. Line and grease a 17 cm (7") cake tin.
2. Take one third of the almond paste and roll it out to a round the size of the cake tin base.
3. Mix the prepared currants, sultanas, peel and cherries with the flour salt and spices. Cream the butter and sugar until pale and fluffy. Add the beaten eggs a little at a time beating well after each addition. Fold in half the flour and fruit using a tablespoon then fold in the rest of the flour mixture. Put half the mixture into the prepared tin.
4. Smooth and cover with the almond paste. Put the remaining cake mixture on top.
5. Bake for 45—50 mins on DUAL COOK (on 160°C microwave LOW).
6. After cooking decorate with the remainder of the almond paste.

Madeira Cake

225 g (8 oz) plain flour
Pinch of salt
2 x 5 ml tsp baking powder
Grated rind of 1 lemon
150 g (5 oz) castor sugar
150 g (5 oz) butter
3 x size 2 eggs
3 x 15 ml tbsp milk
A slice of lemon peel

1. Lightly grease a 18 cm (7″) cake tin.
2. Sieve flour, salt, and baking powder. Add lemon rind.
3. Cream sugar and butter until light and fluffy. Beat in eggs a little at a time.
4. Fold in dry ingredients. Add milk.
5. Place in prepared cake tin, bake for 15—18 mins on DUAL COOK BAKE (on 200°C microwave MEDIUM LOW).

Parkin

175 g (6 oz) plain flour
½ x 5 ml tsp salt
1 x 5 ml tsp each, mixed spice, cinnamon and ground ginger
1 x 5 ml tsp bicarbonate of soda
300 g (10 oz) medium oatmeal
175 g (6 oz) black treacle
150 g (5 oz) butter
100 g (4 oz) soft brown sugar
150 ml (¼ pt) milk
1 size 3 egg, beaten

1. Brush a 18 cm (7″) square cake tin with melted fat, line base and sides with grease-proof paper, brush with more fat.
2. Sift flour, salt, spice, cinnamon, ground ginger, and bicarbonate of soda into a bowl. Add oatmeal. Make a well in the centre.
3. Put treacle, butter, sugar, salt and milk in a heat-proof bowl and MICROWAVE on HIGH for 3 mins.
4. Pour into the well and add the egg. Stir mixture briskly without beating until smooth and evenly combined.
5. Transfer to tin, bake for 14—17 mins on DUAL COOK BAKE (on 200°C microwave MEDIUM LOW).
6. Cool on a wire rack, store without removing paper in an airtight tin for about one week before cutting.

Farmhouse Fruit Cake

225 g (8 oz) self raising flour
100 g (4 oz) butter
100 g (4 oz) soft dark brown sugar
100 g (4 oz) mixed fruit
50 g (2 oz) chopped cherries
1 x 5 ml tsp vanilla essence
2 egg size 3
5 x 15 ml tbsp cold milk
25 g (1 oz) demerara sugar

1. Prepare 18 cm (8″) cake tin.
2. Rub butter into the flour in a large bowl, until the mixture resembles breadcrumbs. Add the sugar, fruit and cherries. Blend well.
3. Stir the eggs and milk into the dry ingredients, add the vanilla essence and beat to a smooth batter.
4. Pour into the prepared tin. Sprinkle with demerara sugar. Bake for 15—18 mins on DUAL COOK BAKE (on 200°C microwave MEDIUM LOW).

Sharp Christmas Cake

100 g (4 oz) walnuts
175 g (6 oz) glace cherries - halved
225 g (8 oz) mixed dried fruit
100 g (4 oz) glace pineapple
100 g (4 oz) candied mixed peel - chopped
225 g (8 oz) butter
225 g (8 oz) dark brown sugar
2 x 15 ml tbsp treacle
50 g (2 oz) ground almonds
4 size 3 eggs
225 g (8 oz) self raising flour
Grated rind and juice of 1 orange
3 x 15 ml tbsp rum

1. Line a 23 cm (9″) cake tin using a double thickness of greaseproof paper.
2. Prepare fruit.
3. Cut the glace pineapple and cherries into small cubes.
4. Cream the butter and sugar until fluffy and stir in the almonds.
5. Add the beaten eggs and black treacle.
6. Coat the fruits and peel in a little of the flour. Fold the fruit followed by the flour, the grated orange rind and the orange juice, into the mixture.
7. Lastly, stir in the rum. Pour the mixture into the tin.
8. Cook for 90—95 mins on DUAL COOK (on 130°C microwave LOW).
9. Cool in the tin and store until required.

Passion Cake

175 ml (6 fl oz) corn oil
175 g (6 oz) castor sugar
3 size 3 eggs
1 x 5 ml tsp vanilla essence
225 g (8 oz) carrots
100 g (4 oz) walnutpieces — chopped
175 g (6 oz) plain flour
1 x 5 ml tsp bicarbonate of soda
1 x 5 ml tsp baking powder
1 x 5 ml tsp cinnamon
1 x 5 ml tsp salt

1. Grease a 22 cm (8½") cake tin.
2. Blend well the oil, sugar, eggs and vanilla essence in a bowl.
3. Add grated carrots, walnuts, flour, bicarbonate of soda, baking powder, salt and cinnamon.
4. Pour the batter into prepared tin and bake for 23—28 mins on DUAL COOK BAKE (on 200°C microwave MEDIUM LOW).

Genoa Cake

100g (4 ozs) candied peel
40g (1½ ozs) almonds
225g (8 ozs) plain flour
Pinch of salt
1 x 5 ml tsp baking powder
Grated lemon rind
225g (8 ozs) sultanas
225g (8 ozs) currants
200g (7 ozs) butter
175g (6 ozs) sugar
3 size 3 eggs
Milk to mix

1. Chop the peel and blanch and chop the almonds, reserving some for decoration.
2. Sieve the dry ingredients, add a little grated lemon rind and the fruit and nuts.
3. Cream the fat and the sugar, add the eggs one at a time and beat.
4. Stir in the dry ingredients lightly with a metal spoon, adding a little milk if necessary to give a dropping consistency.
5. Put into a greased and lined 20 cm (8") tin, place the split almonds on the top and bake for 20—25 mins on DUAL COOK BAKE (on 200°C microwave MEDIUM LOW), or until golden brown and thoroughly cooked.

Chocolate and Walnut Gateaux

100 g (4 oz) butter
100 g (4 oz) castor sugar
100 g (4 oz) self raising flour
75 g (3 oz) ground almonds
50 g (2 oz) cocoa powder
2 eggs, lightly beaten
2 x 15 ml tbsp coffee essence
3 x 15 ml tbsp cold milk
3 x 15 ml tbsp rum
Butter cream filling: 100 g (4 oz) icing sugar
                     50 g (2 oz) butter
                     25 g (1 oz) chopped walnuts

1. Cream together the butter and sugar. Add the beaten eggs slowly.
2. Stir in the dry ingredients, coffee essence and cold milk.
3. Place in a greased 7" cake tin.
4. Bake for 14—17 mins on DUAL COOK BAKE (on 200°C microwave MEDIUM LOW).
5. When cool, split the cake in half and soak with rum.
6. Cream together the icing sugar and butter and walnuts until light and fluffy. Fill the cake and serve.

Orange and Ginger Cake

225 g (8 oz) butter
225 g (8 oz) castor sugar
225 g (8 oz) S.R. Flour
4 size 3 eggs
Rind and juice of 2 large oranges
50 g (2 oz) chopped stem ginger
2 x 5 ml tsp ginger syrup

1. Cream together the butter and sugar until light and fluffy.
2. Gradually stir in the beaten eggs and flour and the rind and juice of the orange and the ginger.
3. Turn mixture into a greased and prepared 18 cm (7") tin.
4. Bake for 15—18 mins on DUAL COOK BAKE (on 200°C microwave MEDIUM LOW).
5. Leave to cool in the tin before turning out and serving.

Chocolate Biscuits

225 g (8 oz) plus 1 x 5 ml tsp
   butter or margarine
100 g (4 oz) castor sugar
225 g (8 oz) self raising flour
50 g (2 oz) cocoa
1 x 5 ml tsp vanilla essence

1. Cream the 225 g (8 oz) butter with a wooden spoon until it is pale and fluffy. Gradually add the sugar and beat with the spoon until the mixture is smooth. Sift in the flour, and cocoa a little at a time, stirring until the mixture is a smooth paste. Stir in the vanilla essence.

2. Roll teaspoons of the paste into balls in your hands and place them on a greased baking sheet. (use the 1 x 5 ml teaspoon of margarine to grease the baking sheet). leaving about 5 cm (2") between each one. Dip a fork in cold water and use the back of the prongs to flatten out the balls.

3. Bake for 14—17 mins on 200°C. Allow to cook slightly before lifting carefully off the sheet. These biscuits can be served plain or sandwich together with a little flavoured butter cream. Store in an airtight tin.

Makes about 25 biscuits.

Peanut Butter Cookies

3 x 15 ml tbsp peanut butter
Grated rind of ½ orange
50 g (2 oz) castor sugar
3 x 15 ml tbsp soft brown sugar
1 x size 3 egg beaten
100g (4 oz) self raising flour

1. Cream peanut butter, rind and sugars until light and fluffy.

2. Add egg and flour, beat well.

3. Take walnut sized pieces of biscuit mixture, roll between your hands, place on an ungreased baking sheet or turntable. Flatten and mark with a fork, dip the fork into flour if the mixture sticks. Bake for 15—17 mins on 200°C.

Rich Shortbread

100 g (4 oz) butter softened
50 g (2 oz) castor sugar
150 g (5 oz) plain flour
25 g (1 oz) semolina
25 g (1 oz) cornflour
castor sugar to dredge

1. Cream butter and sugar together until light and fluffy.

2. Using a fork, gradually stir in flour and semolina and cornflour.

3. Draw the mixture together with finger tips and press lightly into a greased 20—22 cm (8—9") sandwich tin.

4. Prick well all over, and pinch edges with the finger and thumb.

5. Bake for 7—10 mins on DUAL COOK BAKE (on 200°C microwave MEDIUM LOW).

6. Cut into 8 triangles, dredge with castor sugar and roll.

Chocolate Cherry Cookies

100 g (4 oz) butter or margarine
50 g (2 oz) castor sugar
½ x 5 ml tsp vanilla essence
25 g (1 oz) finely chopped cherries
25 g (1 oz) finely chopped plain
   chocolate
100 g (4 oz) plain flour

1. Cream butter and sugar until light and fluffy.

2. Add vanilla essence, cherries, and chocolate mix well.

3. Fold flour into mixture. Lightly butter, turntable and baking sheet. Place 18 — 20 teaspoonfulls of mixture well apart on the turntable bake for 15—17 mins on 200°C, until golden brown. Leave for 5 mins before removing.

Viennese Fingers

225 g (8 oz) butter
50 g (2 oz) icing sugar
325 g (11 oz) plain flour
2 egg yolks
4 drops of vanilla essence
100 g (4 oz) plain chocolate

1. Beat the butter until soft in a bowl. Add the sifted icing sugar and a little of the sifted flour and beat.
2. Gradually sift the remaining flour beating well each time.
3. Beat in the egg yolks and vanilla essence.
4. Place in a piping bag with a large star nozzle. Pipe onto baking sheets making each finger about 7.5 cm (3") long.
5. Bake for 14—17 mins on 200°C.
6. Leave to cool.
7. Place the chocolate in a bowl and cook on HIGH for 1—1½ mins then beat well. Dip each end of the fingers in the chocolate and allow to cool on a wire rack.
8. Store in an airtight container.

Easter Biscuits

100 g (4 oz) butter or margarine
100 g (4 oz) sugar
1 x size 3 egg yolk
225 g (8 oz) plain flour
2 x 5 ml tsp grated lemon rind

1. Cream the margarine until light and fluffy, stir in the sugar and beat until smooth and creamy. Beat in the egg yolk. Stir in the flour and lemon rind. Add a little lemon juice if required. Using hands form the mixture into a ball and knead lightly. Cover and chill in the refrigerator for 10 mins.
2. Roll out on a lightly floured surface until ½ cm thick. Using a 2½" (6 cm) cutter cut out and place on a lightly greased baking sheet.
3. Cook for 14—18 mins on 200°C until golden brown round the edges. Cool on a wire rack. Store in an airtight tin.

Ginger Biscuits

50 g (2 oz) margarine
50 g (2 oz) castor sugar
1 x 15 ml tbsp black treacle
100 g (4 oz) self raising flour
1 x 5 ml tsp ground ginger
¼ x 5 ml tsp mixed spice
Milk to mix

1. Cream the margarine and sugar together until light and fluffy. Beat in the treacle. Sieve the flour, ginger and spice onto the mixture. Fold in with a metal spoon and add a little milk if necessary. Turn onto a floured board and knead well. Roll out thinly and cut out with a cutter.
2. Place on a greased baking tray and cook for 15—17 mins on 200°C. Leave on the tray for 3 — 4 mins before putting onto a cooling tray .

Makes approximately 25.

Shrewsbury Biscuits

225 g (8 oz) butter
225 g (8 oz) castor sugar
2 egg beaten
450 g (1 lb) plain flour
2 x 5 ml tsp lemon juice

1. Cream the butter and sugar until fluffy. Add the eggs slowly beating after each addition.
2. Stir in the flour and lemon juice and mix to a firm dough. Roll out to 0.6 cm (¼'') thick. Cut into rounds 6.3 cm (2½'') place on trays.
3. Bake for 15—18 mins on 200°C.

Variation on This Basic Dough

Fruit Biscuits

100 g (4 oz) currants added to the mixture with the flour.

Spice Biscuits

Omit the lemon juice and add 1 x 5 ml tsp mixed spice and 1 tsp ground cinnamon to the flour.

Orange Biscuits

Replace the lemon juice with the juice of one orange.

Cherry Biscuits

Omit the lemon juice and add 50 g (2 oz) chopped glace cherries with the flour.

Swiss Tarts

100 g (4 oz) butter or margarine
25 g (1 oz) castor or icing sugar
Vanilla essence
100 g (4 oz) plain flour
a little jam

1. Cream the margarine and sugar together until light and fluffy. Add a few drops of vanilla essence and beat in half of the flour, mixing well. Beat in the remaining flour until the mxture is well blended. Put the mixture into a piping bag with a large star rozzle and pipe the mixture into paper cases. Start at the centre and pipe round the sides so that a depression is left in the centre. Put onto a baking sheet and stand on the baking trivet.
2. Bake for 14—17 mins on 200°C.
3. Fill the centres with a little jam.

Makes about 7 tarts.

Basic Microwave Cake

175 g (6 oz) margarine
175 g (6 oz) castor sugar
175 g (6 oz) self-raising flour
3 x size 3 eggs
½ x 5 ml tsp baking powder
¼ x 5 ml tsp vanilla essence
3 x 15 ml tbsp milk

1. Line the base of a 18 x 10 cm (7¼ x 4") round container with a circle of greaseproof paper. Do not grease.

2. Cream margarine and sugar until light and fluffy. Beat in eggs and add sifted flour and baking powder alternately with the vanilla essence and milk.

3. Pour into prepared container. Cook on HIGH for 5—6 mins or until cocktail stick is clean when cake tested.

4. Leave in container for 5 mins before turning onto a cooling rack.

Variations:

Chocolate— Substitute 25 g (1 oz) of flour for 25 g (1 oz) of cocoa.

Coffee— Dissolve 2 x 5 ml tsp instant coffee in the water.

Cherry— Add 50 g (2 oz) chopped cherries to flour.

Walnut— Add 50 g (2 oz) chopped walnuts.

The above quantities may be varied.
75 g (3 oz) mixture HIGH 2½—3 min.
100 g (4 oz) mixture
            HIGH 3½—4 mins.

Walnut and Honey Cake

175 g (6 oz) margarine
100 g (4 oz) dark soft brown sugar
50 g (2 oz) clear honey
3 eggs - size 3 - beaten
225 g (8 oz) self raising flour
100 g (4 oz) chopped walnuts
4 x 15 ml tbsp milk

1. Cream margarine, sugar and honey together gently. Gradually add eggs. Blend well.

2. Fold in flour and nuts. Mix to a soft consistency with milk. Spoon into a 20 cm (8") cake dish. Cook for 14—18 mins on DUAL COOK BAKE (on 200°C microwave MEDIUM LOW) until cocktail stick inserted comes out clean.

Ginger Cake

150 ml (¼ pt) milk
1 x 5 ml tsp bicarbonate of soda
100 g (4 oz) butter or margarine
100 g (4 oz) golden syrup
100 g (4 oz) black treacle
75 g (3 oz) soft brown sugar
100 g (4 oz) self-raising flour
100 g (4 oz) wholewheat flour
1 x 5 ml tsp mixed spice
2 x 15 ml tbsp ground ginger
Pinch salt
2 x size 3 eggs

1. Line the base of a 20 cm (8") cake dish with a circle of greaseproof paper.

2. Pour milk and bicarbonate of soda into a dish, heat on HIGH for ½ min.

3. Place butter, syrup, treacle and sugar in a bowl and heat on HIGH for 1½ min, until fat has melted and sugar dissolved.

4. Place flours, spices and salt in a large bowl, stir in treacle mixture and warmed milk. Beat until smooth. Add eggs and beat well.

5. Pour into prepared dish and cook for 13—17 mins on DUAL COOK BAKE (on 200°C microwave MEDIUM LOW) until cocktail stick comes out clean when inserted.

Chocolate Brownies

50 g (2 oz) chocolate
75 g (3 oz) butter
175 g (6 oz) soft brown sugar
2 eggs - size 3
175 g (6 oz) plain flour
¼ x 5 ml baking powder
1 x 5 ml tsp vanilla essence
2 x 15 ml tbsp cold milk

1. Place chocolate and butter in glass bowl. Melt on HIGH for 2 mins, stir.

2. Beat in sugar and eggs until mixture is smooth.

3. Add flour sifted with baking powder, vanilla essence and milk.

4. Spread in a greased glass dish (10 x 6½ x 2") (25 x 16¼ x 5 cm).

5. Bake for 8—12 mins on DUAL COOK BAKE (on 200°C microwave MEDIUM LOW).

6. Allow to stand for 5 mins and dust the top with sifted icing sugar.

Celebration Banana Cake

100 g (4 oz) butter
275 g (10 oz) light brown sugar
2 eggs beaten
350 g (12 oz) self raising flour
¾ x 15 ml tbsp bicarbonate of soda
2 bananas, mashed
3 x 15 ml tbsp natural yoghurt

Filling

2 bananas, mashed
300 ml (½ pt) double cream
lemon juice
chopped walnuts

1. Prepare two 20 cm (8'') cake tins.

2. Cream together bananas and yoghurt.

3. Cream the sugar and butter until pale and fluffy. Add the eggs and mix.

4. Sift the sifted flour, and bicarbonate of soda and salt.

5. Add the mashed bananas and yoghurt mixture.

6. Divide the mixture between the two cake tins.

7. Bake for 15 — 20 mins on DUAL COOK BAKE (on 200°C microwave MEDIUM LOW). Halfway through cooking swop the two layers around.

8. Allow to cool then fill with the mixed double cream mashed banana, lemon juice and chopped nuts.

Breads and Scones
Bread Techniques

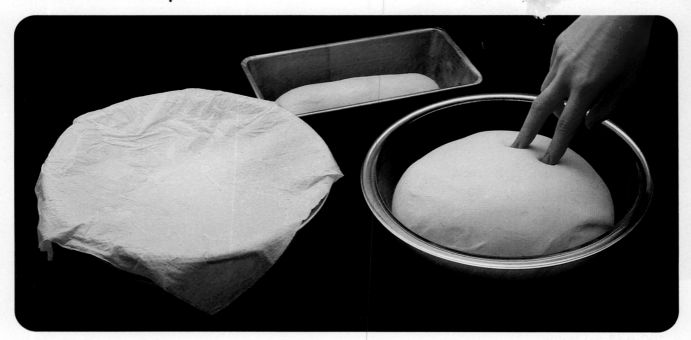

Proving dough. Use your own recipe or frozen dough. Place in well-greased bowl or loaf pan; cover with damp cloth. Set oven on PROOF (40°C) for 30 mins. Most dough will double in 30 min. If not, let stand in oven or reset PROOF (40°C) for 30 mins, continue until ready. Dough is doubled when impressions remain after fingers are pressed 1.2 cm into dough.

Milk Bread

1 x 5 ml tsp sugar
15 g (½ oz) fresh yeast
300 ml (½ pt) hand hot milk
450 g (1 lb) strong plain flour
1 x 5 ml tsp salt
40 g (1½ oz) butter

1. Dissolve the sugar and yeast in half the milk. Sift the flour and salt into a bowl rub in the butter, then make a well in the centre. Pour in the yeast liquid and the remaining milk and mix into a pliable dough.

2. Turn the dough out onto a floured surface and knead for 10 mins until smooth.

3. Put the dough into a lightly greased polythene bag and leave in a warm place until doubled in bulk, or put into a bowl and prove on the proof cycle. (40°C, 30 mins)

4. Shape the dough into an oblong and place into the greased 900 g (2 lb) loaf tin.

5. Bake for 11—15 mins on DUAL COOK BAKE (on 200°C microwave MEDIUM LOW).

Quick Wholemeal Rolls

300 ml (½ pt) water (approx.)
1 x 5 ml tsp sugar
450 g (1 lb) wholemeal flour
2 x 5 ml tsp salt
25 g (1 oz) lard
15 g (½ oz) fresh yeast

1. Activate the yeast in 150 ml (¼ pint) of the water with the sugar. Mix the flour and salt and rub in the fat.

2. Add the yeast mixture and remaining water and mix to a fairly soft dough, adding more water if necessary.

3. Beat and knead well and divide into 10—12 portions shape into rolls. Prove on proof cycle for 30 mins. (40°C, 30 mins.)

4. Bake for 12—16 mins on DUAL COOK BAKE (on 200°C microwave MEDIUM LOW) until brown.

Walnut and Cherry Tea Bread

75 g (3 oz) butter
75 g (3 oz) castor sugar
1 egg beaten
350 g (12 oz) plain flour
4 level 5 ml tsp baking powder
1 x 5 ml tsp mixed spice
1 tsp salt
100 g (4 oz) walnuts
100 g (4 oz) glace cherries
300 ml (½ pt) fresh milk
2 x 15 ml tbsp honey, warmed

1. Cream butter and sugar together until light and fluffy, beat in the eggs gradually.

2. Sift dry ingredients together. Chop 50 g (2 oz) each of the walnuts and cherries and add to the dry ingredients.

3. Fold flour mixture and milk alternately into butter and sugar mixture to make a smooth batter.

4. Pour flour mixture into a greased and lined 1 kg (2 lb) loaf or cake tin. Halve the remaining nuts and cherries and sprinkle over top of loaf.

5. Bake for 15—18 mins on DUAL COOK BAKE (on 200°C microwave MEDIUM LOW).

Hot Cross Buns

25 g (1 oz) fresh yeast or 1 tbsp (20ml) dried yeast
75 g (3 oz) castor sugar
450 g (1 lb) strong plain flour
½ x 5 ml tsp salt
½ x 5 ml tsp ground nutmeg
1 x 5 ml tsp ground cinnamon
1 x 5 ml tsp mixed spice
75 g (3 oz) margarine
1 egg beaten made up to 250 ml (½ pt) with milk and water
100 g (4 oz) currants
50 g (2 oz) chopped mixed peel

Paste

25 g (1 oz) margarine
50 g (2 oz) plain flour
4 x 15 ml tbsp water

Glaze

40 g (1½ oz) castor sugar
75 ml (3fl oz) milk and water

1. Froth the dried yeast in the warm liquid with 1 x 5 ml tsp of the sugar, or crumble the fresh yeast into the warm liquid.
2. Sift the remaining sugar, flour, salt and spices together and rub in the margarine. Make a well in the centre of the flour mixture and pour in the yeast liquid and mix to form a dough.
3. Knead the dough until smooth and elastic. Place in a bowl cover and prove until double in size on the proof cycle. (40°C, 30 mins)
4. Add the fruit and re-knead. Divide the dough into 12 pieces and shape into buns. Place well apart on greased baking sheets. Prove again for 15 mins on the proof cycle. (40°C, 15 mins)
5. To make paste mix all ingredients together well and place in a piping bag with a small plain nozzle. Cut crosses on the buns and then pipe the paste.
6. Bake for 14—18 mins on DUAL COOK BAKE (on 200°C microwave MEDIUM LOW). Halfway through cooking swop the two layers around. When the buns have cooked place on cooling rack. Make the glaze and brush the buns with the hot glaze leave to cool.

Chelsea Buns

50 g (2 oz) strong plain flour
15 g (½ oz) fresh yeast or 2 x 5ml tsp dried yeast
100 ml (4fl oz) warm milk
175 g (6 oz) strong plain flour
½ x 5 ml tsp salt
½ x 5 ml tsp castor sugar
15 g (½ oz) butter or margarine
1 egg beaten

Filling

50 g (2 oz) butter, melted
75 g (3 oz) dried fruit
25 g (1 oz) mixed peel
50 g (2 oz) soft brown sugar

Glaze

honey

1. Blend 50 g (2 oz) flour, the yeast and milk together in a large bowl and put to one side for 20 mins until the mixture froths.
2. Sieve the flour, salt and sugar and rub in the fat. Then make a well in the centre and pour in the yeast batter, beaten egg and beat until a soft dough forms.
3. Knead until smooth and elastic. Cover and prove on proof cycle. (40°C, 30 mins)
4. Knead the dough and roll to a rectangle 30cm x 22.5cm (12" x 9"). Brush the surface with melted butter and then sprinkle with the fruit peel and sugar.
5. Roll up from the longest side, like a Swiss Roll. Cut into nine equal slices and place in a 18 cm (7") square tin. Cover and prove for 15 mins on the proof cycle. (40°C, 15 mins)
6. Bake for 14—18 mins on DUAL COOK (on 230°C microwave LOW).
7. Cool on a wire rack brush with honey.

Danish Tea Ring

Bread Mixture
7.5 g (¼ oz) fresh yeast or
1 x 5 ml tsp dried yeast
½ x 5 ml tsp sugar
100 ml (4fl oz) warm milk
50 g (2 oz) strong plain flour
25 g (1 oz) margarine
150 g (6 oz) strong plain flour
½ x 5 ml tsp salt
1 small egg

Filling
50 g (2 oz) sugar
50 g (2 oz) ground almonds
few drops almond essence
1 egg white
15 g (½ oz) butter melted

Frosting
75 g (3 oz) icing sugar
1 x 5 ml tsp lemon juice
2 x 5 ml tsp water
3—4 glace cherries
angelica

1. Froth the yeast in the sugar and milk plus 50 g (2 oz) flour for 20 mins.

2. Rub the margarine into the remaining flour. Add the yeast batter together with the egg and beat until smooth. Place in a bowl cover and prove on the proof cycle (40°C) for 30 mins until double in bulk.

3. Prepare filling by mixing sugar, ground almonds and almond essence together, adding enough egg white to form a soft paste.

4. Roll the dough to a rectangle 20cm x 35cm (8" x 14"). Brush with melted butter and spread filling over. Roll up tightly to form a long roll.

5. Place on a greased baking sheet and curve the ends round to form a ring.

6. Make cut half to three quarters way through the dough with scissors at an angle about 2.5 cm (1") apart. Fan out sections on their sides. Cover and prove (40°C) for about 30—35 mins.

7. Bake for 12—16 mins on DUAL COOK (on 220°C microwave LOW).

8. To prepare icing sieve the icing sugar into a bowl. Add the lemon juice and sufficient water to make an icing of a fairly firm consistency. Spoon over the top of the cooled tea ring and decorate with cherries and angelica.

Date and Nut Bread

100 g (4 oz) chopped walnuts
225 g (8 oz) chopped dates
1 x 5 ml tsp baking soda
½ x 5 ml tsp salt
3 x 15 ml tbsp margarine or butter
200 ml (⅓ pt) boiling water
225 g (8 oz) soft brown sugar
½ x 5 ml tsp vanilla essence
175 g (6 oz) plain flour
2 eggs size 3

1. Lightly grease a 450 g (1 lb) loaf dish. Combine walnuts, dates, baking soda and salt in large bowl. Add margarine and boiling water. Stir lightly and allow to stand for 20 mins.

2. Add sugar and vanilla essence, and stir well. Then add sifted flour and lightly beaten eggs, and mix well. Pour batter into loaf dish. Place loaf dish on inverted sauce in oven.

3. Cook for 50—60 mins on 180°C. Let stand for 5 mins. Remove from loaf dish, and serve warm or cold with butter.

Soda Bread

100 g (4 oz) wholemeal flour
175 g (6 oz) plain flour
½ x 5 ml tsp salt
1 x 5 ml tsp bicarbonate of soda
2 x 5 ml tsp cream of tartar
25 g (1 oz) margarine
150 ml (¼ pt) milk

1. Sift all dry ingredients into a bowl. Rub in margarine finely.

2. Mix with milk to form a soft but not sticky dough. Knead lightly. Place on large dinner plate, pat out into a circle approx. 20 cm (8") diameter.

3. Divide into 8 wedges and almost cut through with a knife. Cook for 13—18 mins on DUAL COOK (on 230°C microwave LOW). Eat on day of making. Makes 8 portions.

675g (1½ lb) wholemeal flour
15g (½ oz) lard
1 x 15 ml tbsp castor sugar
15g (½ oz) dried yeast
450 ml (¾ pt) water, hand hot
2 x 5 ml tsp salt

1. Place flour in a non metal bowl, heat on HIGH in Microwave for 1 min. Rub lard into flour.
2. Sprinkle one tsp sugar and yeast into 150 ml (¼ pt) of water. Leave in a warm place for 10—15 mins until the mixture is frothy. Pour remaining sugar and salt into water. Add to flour with yeast mixture. Knead for 5 mins until dough is smooth and elastic. Cover dough with polythene bag, leave in a warm place for 30 mins or until doubled in size. Knead for a further 5 mins, divide into two. Shape and place in two greased 1 kg (2 lb) loaf tins. Leave in a warm place until dough has doubled in size. Bake for 12—16 mins on DUAL COOK BAKE (on 200°C microwave MEDIUM LOW).

Apricot Tea Bread

50 g (2 oz) dried apricots, chopped
150 g (5 oz) sultanas
150 ml (¼ pt) warm tea
100 g (4 oz) demerara sugar
1 x size 3 egg
225 g (8 oz) plain flour
1 x 5 ml tsp baking powder
½ x 5 ml tsp mixed spice
½ x 5 ml tsp salt
Topping: 1½ x 15 ml tbsp apricot
jam, 25 g (1 oz) sultanas

1. Place apricots in large bowl with sultanas, warm tea and demerara sugar. Mix together. Cook, covered on HIGH for 5—6½ mins, leave to cool 10 mins.

2. Lightly grease a 1.7-litre (3 pt) dish. Stir egg into fruit mixture. Sift flour, spice and salt together. Add to fruit mixture, mix well, use little more warm tea if mixture is very stiff. Place mixture into prepared dish and level top.

3. Cook for 40—50 mins on 180°C, turn out, leave to cool on wire rack.

4. To make topping, place apricot jam in a small bowl, warm on HIGH for ½—¾ min. Add sultanas and mix thoroughly. Spread topping over tea bread and leave to cool. Serve sliced and buttered.

Note: Tea bread will improve in flavour if stored in a tin. Store up to 4 weeks.

To freeze: wrap in plastic film and foil without topping for up to 3 months.

Malt Loaf

350 g (12 oz) self raising flour
40 g (1½ oz) soft brown sugar
75 g (3 oz) seedless raisins
40 g (1½ oz) walnuts, finely chopped
40 g (1½ oz) black treacle
75 g (3 oz) malt extract
225 ml (8fl oz) fresh milk

1. Sift the flour into a mixing bowl, add the sugar, raisins and walnuts.

2. Blend together the treacle, malt extract and milk on microwave HIGH for 2—3 mins. Stir gradually into the flour and beat until smooth.

3. Spoon the mixture into a greased and floured 1 kg (2 lb) loaf tin and smooth over the top.

4. Cook for 20—25 mins on DUAL COOK BAKE (on 200°C microwave MEDIUM LOW).

Banana bread

200 g (7 oz) plain flour
½ x 5 ml tsp baking powder
½ x 5 ml tsp bicarbonate of soda
½ x 5 ml tsp salt
2—3 mashed ripe bananas
1 x 15 ml tbsp lemon juice
75 g (3 oz) softened butter or margarine
150 g (5 oz) sugar
2 eggs size 3
70 ml (3 fl oz) milk
35 g (1½ oz) coarsely broken walnuts

1. Lightly grease a 21½ cm x 11 cm x 6 cm (8½" x 4½" x 2½") loaf dish. Sift together flour, baking powder, bicarbonate of soda and salt. In a small bowl, combine mashed banana and lemon juice.

2. In a large bowl, cream butter and sugar together until light and fluffy. Add eggs, one at a time, beating well after each addition.

3. Add milk and dry ingredients alternately, beginning and ending with dry ingredients. Fold in walnuts and banana mixture.

4. Pour batter into prepared dish and place in oven on an inverted saucer. Cook for 40—50 mins on 180°C. Cool in dish, 10 mins.

Crisp Bread Rolls

675 g (1½ lb) strong white flour
2 x 5 ml tsp salt
1 x 15 ml tbsp lard
2 x 5 ml tsp dried yeast
1 x 5 ml tsp castor sugar
450 ml (¾ pt) milk and water

1. Sift flour and salt together into a large mixing bowl. Cut lard into small pieces and rub into flour.

2. Stir sugar into milk and water. Heat on HIGH for 1½—2 mins until the mixture is hand hot. Sprinkle yeast into liquid. Leave for 10 mins or until the mixture is frothy.

3. Make a well in the centre of the flour, pour in the yeast liquid. Combine all ingredients into a ball. Knead well for 10 mins. Place in a greased bowl, cover with a damp cloth, leave in a warm place until the dough has doubled in size, approximately 1 hour.

4. Knead dough for a further 5 mins. Divide mixture into 12 pieces. Shape into rolls and place on turntable or baking sheet. Leave again in a warm place until the rolls have doubled in size. Brush with salted water.

5. Bake for 18—22 mins on DUAL COOK BAKE (on 200°C microwave MEDIUM LOW). Alternate the two layers halfway through cooking.

Challah (Jewish Eggbread)

15 g (½ oz) fresh yeast or
2 x 5 ml tsp dried yeast
2 x 5 ml tsp castor sugar
200 ml (8 fl oz) warm water
450 g (1 lb) plain flour
1 x 5 ml tsp salt
2 eggs, beaten

1. Froth the dried yeast in the warm water together with ½ x 5 ml tsp castor sugar, or crumble the fresh yeast into the warm water.

2. Add 150 g (6 oz) of the flour to the yeast liquid and mix until well blended.

3. Cover with a damp cloth and leave for 1 hour or until doubled in bulk.

4. Add the remaining flour, salt and sugar with the eggs to the risen dough and knead for 10 mins.

5. Cover with a damp cloth and leave in a warm place until double in bulk.

6. Re-knead the dough and divide into three equal pieces.

7. Plait these to form a loaf, moisten the ends with water and press together.

8. Place on a greased baking sheet.

9. Cover with a damp cloth and leave in warm place until doubled in bulk.

10. Brush with the glaze and sprinkle with poppy seeds.

11. Bake for 12—17 mins on DUAL COOK BAKE (on 200°C microwave MEDIUM LOW).

Fruit Scones

225 g (8 oz) S.R. Flour
50 g (2 oz) margarine
150 ml (¼ pt) milk
Pinch of salt, pinch of cream of tartar
25 g (1 oz) sugar
75 g (3 oz) currants

1. Sieve together the flour, salt and cream of tartar.

2. Rub fat into the flour, add the sugar and the dried fruit.

3. Add the milk until a soft consistency, form gently into a ball.

4. Roll out the dough and cut into rounds about 1 cm (½") deep.

5. Place on a greased baking sheet and glaze with beaten egg or milk. Cook for 10—14 mins on DUAL COOK (on 230°C microwave LOW).

Short Bread

100 g (4 oz) butter
50 g (2 oz) castor sugar or soft brown sugar
150 g (5 oz) plain flour
25 g (1 oz) semolina or ground rice

1. Cream butter and sugar, gradually work in the flour and semolina or ground rice with a fork. Knead well.

2. Press out into a 18 cm (7") plate. Crimp edges with fingers, and prick with a fork.

3. Heat on HIGH for 2½—3½ mins. Cut into wedges and cool.

Cheese Scones

200 g (8 oz) self raising flour
40 g (1½ oz) butter or margarine
75 g (3 oz) cheese, finely grated
1 x 5 ml tsp mustard
150 ml (¼ pt) milk (approx.)

1. Grease a baking tray.
2. Mix the flour and salt and rub in the fat until the mixture resembles fine breadcrumbs.
3. Stir in half the cheese, mustard and enough milk to give a fairly soft, light dough.
4. Roll out about 2 cm (¾'') thick and cut into rounds.
5. Place on baking tray and sprinkle with the other half of the cheese.
6. Cook for 10—14 mins on DUAL COOK (on 230°C microwave LOW).

Honey Scones

225 g (½ lb) self raising flour
1 x 2.5 ml spoon/½ x 5 ml tsp mixed spice
2 x 5 ml tsp castor sugar
50 g (2 oz) butter
2 x 15 ml tbsp honey
6 x 15 ml tbsp milk

1. Sift the flour and spice into a bowl, stir in the sugar and rub in the butter until the mixture resembles fine breadcrumbs.
2. Add half the honey and the milk and mix to a soft dough.
3. Turn the dough out onto a floured surface, knead until smooth.
4. Roll out to 2 cm (¾'') thickness. Cut about 10—12 rounds with a 5cm (2'') cutter.
5. Place on a greased baking sheet.
6. Cook for 10—14 mins on DUAL COOK (on 230°C microwave LOW).

INDEX

MEMO

MEMO

MEMO

MEMO

Food

ORANGES

Louise Spilsbury

Heinemann
LIBRARY

H www.heinemann.co.uk/library
Visit our website to find out more information about Heinemann Library books.

To order:
☎ Phone 44 (0) 1865 888066
🖹 Send a fax to 44 (0) 1865 314091
🖥 Visit the Heinemann Bookshop at www.heinemann.co.uk/library to browse our catalogue and order online.

First published in Great Britain by Heinemann Library,
Halley Court, Jordan Hill, Oxford OX2 8EJ
a division of Reed Educational and Professional Publishing Ltd.
Heinemann is a registered trademark of Reed Educational and Professional Publishing Ltd.

OXFORD MELBOURNE AUCKLAND
JOHANNESBURG BLANTYRE GABORONE
IBADAN PORTSMOUTH (NH) USA CHICAGO

Designed by Celia Floyd
Illustrated by Alan Fraser and Jeff Edwards
Originated by Ambassador Litho Ltd
Printed in Hong Kong/China by South China Printing Co.

ISBN 0 431 12772 7 (hardback)
06 05 04 03 02
10 9 8 7 6 5 4 3 2 1

British Library Cataloguing in Publication Data
Spilsbury, Louise
    Oranges. – (Food)
    1. Oranges 2. Juvenile literature
    I. Title
    641.3'431

Acknowledgements
The Publishers would like to thank the following for permission to reproduce photographs:
Corbis: pp.5, 7, 8, 12, 16, 9; Holt Studios International: pp.11, 14, 17; Liz Eddison: pp.4, 23, 28, 29 (top and bottom); Richard Spilsbury: p.24; Photodisc: p.13; Pictor International: p.15; Sequoia: pp.18, 19, 20, 21; Stone: p.25; Telegraph Colour Library: p.22; Visuals Unlimited: Eric Anderson, p.6.

Cover photograph reproduced with permission of Gareth Boden.

Every effort has been made to contact copyright holders of any material reproduced in this book. Any omissions will be rectified in subsequent printings if notice is given to the Publishers.

CONTENTS

Words written in bold, **like this**, are explained in the Glossary.

WHAT ARE ORANGES?

Oranges are a kind of **citrus fruit**.
Lemons and limes are citrus fruits too.
People eat more oranges than any
other citrus fruit in the world.

Oranges, like other citrus fruits, grow on trees. A group of orange trees growing together is called a **grove**. This orange grove is in the USA.

KINDS OF ORANGES

Navel, Valencia and blood oranges are sweet oranges. We take the **peel** off sweet oranges and eat the fruit inside **raw**.

Valencia orange   blood orange   Navel orange

6

Seville oranges are **sour**. They are not sweet so we do not eat them raw. People cook them with sugar to make **marmalade**.

IN THE PAST

The first orange trees grew in Asia. Alexander the Great was a Greek king. His army travelled far. He brought oranges from Asia to Europe over 2000 years ago.

Christopher Columbus was the first person from Europe to go to America. In 1493 he planted **seeds** to grow the first orange trees there.

AROUND THE WORLD

This map of the world shows the places that grow most oranges today. Oranges grow best where it is very hot in summer and chilly in winter.

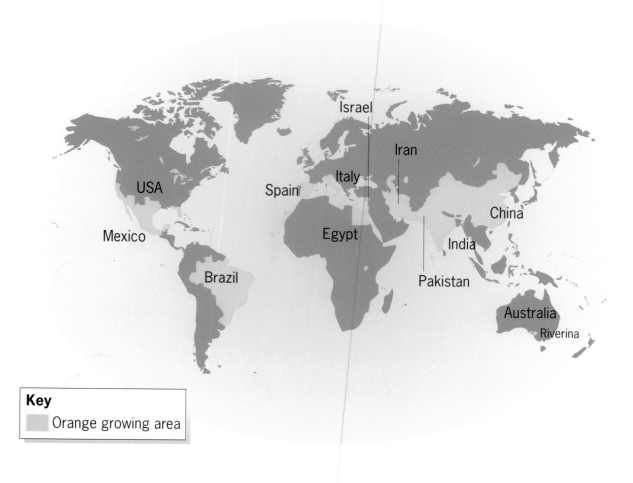

Israel

Iran

Italy

USA

Spain

China

Mexico

Egypt

India

Brazil

Pakistan

Australia

Riverina

Key

Orange growing area

Oranges also need plenty of water to grow well. In countries where there is not enough rain, **irrigation channels** give the trees the water they need.

LOOKING AT ORANGES

Orange trees have shiny green leaves and white flowers. They grow on branches from a tall **trunk**. The tree's **roots** are underground.

leaves

branch

trunk

roots
(underground)

Most oranges are round and have a thick orange-coloured **peel**. The peel protects the **flesh** inside. The white bits are called **pith**. Some oranges have pips (**seeds**).

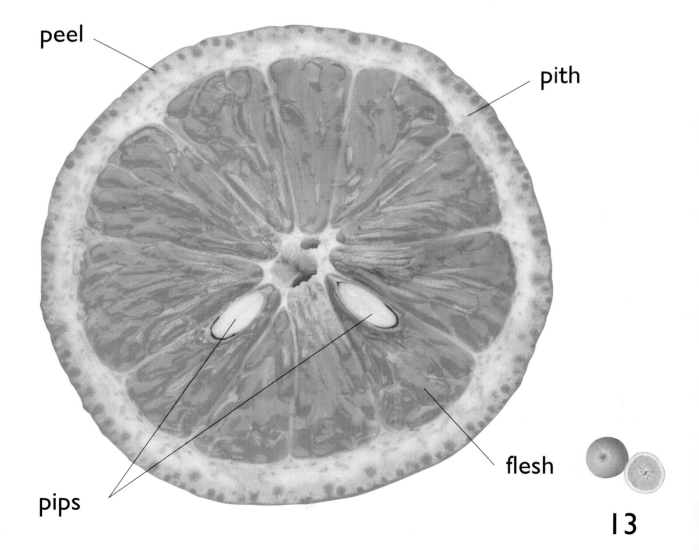

peel

pith

pips

flesh

PICKING ORANGES

Most orange trees grow flowers in spring. After a while the flowers die and drop off. Oranges grow in place of some of the flowers.

The oranges grow on the trees until they are **ripe** (ready to eat). Workers pick the ripe oranges by hand. They are careful not to damage the fruits.

CHECKING AND WASHING

Workers put the oranges into big tubs. A machine lifts the tubs and tips the oranges into trailers. These take the oranges to a **packing house**.

At the packing house workers check the oranges. They throw away bad or damaged ones. A machine washes the fruit to get rid of dust and dirt.

WAXING AND SORTING

Oranges are covered with a very thin layer of natural **wax**. Washing rubs this off. Machines put a new layer on. This helps to keep the oranges fresh.

Next, the oranges are sorted by size. A camera takes pictures to see how big they are. Then the oranges are sorted into different sizes.

LABELS AND PACKING

Another machine puts a little sticker onto every orange. The sticker tells you what sort of orange it is and where it comes from.

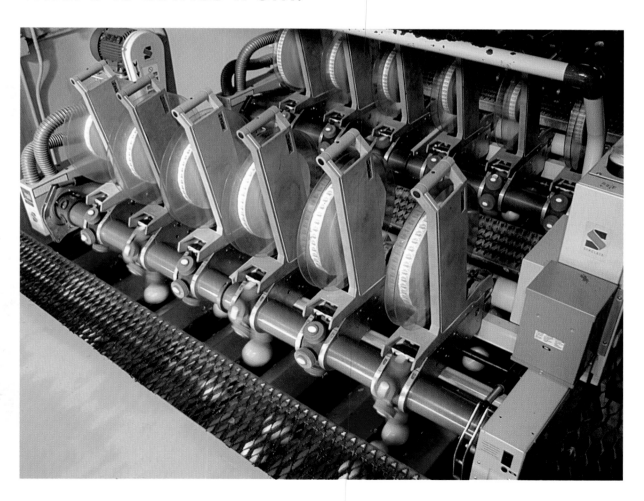

Packing machines put the oranges into boxes. Some oranges are sold in the country where they grew. Others are **exported** (sold to other countries).

EATING ORANGES

Many oranges are made into orange juice. In a **factory**, machines squeeze the oranges to get the juice out. Then they put it into cartons or bottles.

Oranges are used to make
marmalade to spread on toast.
Oranges are also used to flavour
cakes and muffins, and other foods.

23

GOOD FOR YOU

Oranges are rich in **vitamins**.
Vitamins help your body to grow and
they protect you from illness.

Oranges also contain **fibre**. Fibre is a part of some foods that passes through your body when you eat it. It helps keep your body healthy.

HEALTHY EATING

You need to eat different kinds of food to keep you well. This food pyramid shows you how much of each different food you need.

You should eat some of the things at the bottom and in the middle of the pyramid every day. Sweet foods are at the top of the pyramid. Try not to eat too many of these!

The food in each part of the pyramid helps your body in different ways.

Oranges belong in the middle of the pyramid.

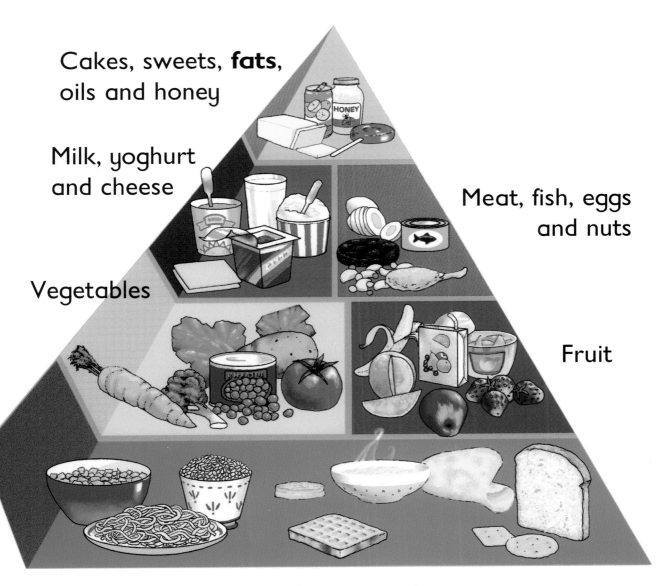

Cakes, sweets, **fats**, oils and honey

Milk, yoghurt and cheese

Meat, fish, eggs and nuts

Vegetables

Fruit

Bread, **cereals**, rice and pasta

ORANGE SMOOTHIE RECIPE

1 Peel the bananas and cut it into pieces.

2 Chop the strawberries into pieces.

Ask an adult to help you!

You will need:
- 1 cup of orange juice
- 1 cup of fresh or frozen strawberries
- 2 fresh bananas

3 Pour the orange juice into a blender.

4 Add the strawberries and bananas. Ask an adult to blend them until smooth.

5 Pour the smoothie into two tall glasses. Decorate with an orange slice and a strawberry, if you like.

GLOSSARY

cereals grains like wheat and rice that are used to make flour, bread and breakfast foods

citrus fruit kind of fruit that grows on citrus trees. Citrus fruits have thick peel, pulpy flesh and you can eat them. Oranges, limes, lemons and grapefruits are citrus fruits.

exported when food or other goods are taken from one country to be sold in another country

factory large building where things are made, such as toys or shoes, or food and drinks

fats type of food. Butter, oil and margarine are kinds of fat.

fibre part of a plant that passes through our bodies when we eat it

flesh part of some fruits that we can eat. The flesh is inside the peel or rind.

grove piece of land where orange trees are grown. They are often planted in rows.

irrigation channels passages that a farmer creates to get water from one place to another. They supply water to the groves. This water helps the oranges trees to grow.

marmalade kind of jam made from oranges and sugar

packing house building where fruit or other goods are sorted and packed. Then they are ready to be taken to the shops to be sold.

peel skin or rind of a fruit like an orange

pith white bits in a fruit like an orange

raw not cooked

ripe when a fruit is ready to eat

roots part of a plant under the ground. Roots hold the plant firmly in the ground. They also take in water from the soil for the plant.

seeds made by flowers. They are released from a plant and grow into a new plant.

sour not sweet

trunk stem of a tree. Trunks hold up the branches with their leaves and flowers to get the warmth and light the tree needs to grow.

vitamins food contains vitamins. Vitamins help us grow and protect our bodies from illness.

wax fatty stuff made by some plants and animals. You cannot see the layer of wax on oranges, but it helps to stop the fruit drying out.

MORE BOOKS TO READ

Plants: Flowers, Fruits and Seeds, Angela Royston, Heinemann Library, 1999

Safe and Sound: Eat Well, Angela Royston, Heinemann Library, 1999

Senses: Tasting, Karen Hartley, Chris Macro, Phillip Taylor, Heinemann Library, 2000

The Senses: Taste, Mandy Suhr, Hodder Wayland, 1994

INDEX

Titles in the *Food* series include:

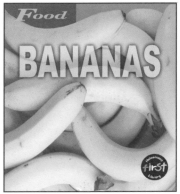

Hardback   0 431 12770 0

Hardback   0 431 12700 X

Hardback   0 431 12771 9

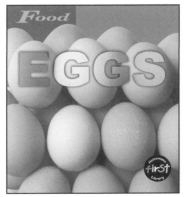

Hardback   0 431 12702 6

Hardback   0 431 12706 9

Hardback   0 431 12701 8

Hardback   0 431 12772 7

Hardback   0 431 12773 5

Find out about the other titles in this series on our website www.heinemann.co.uk/library